MW00397443

Coordination Abilities of Youth and Adult Athletes

By

Vladimir B. Issurin, PhD, Professor
Wingate Institute for Physical Education and Sport
Israel

Vladimir I. Lyakh, PhD, Professor
University School of Physical Education in Cracow
Poland

Coordination Abilities of youth and adult athletes

By

Vladimir B. Issurin, PhD. & Vladimir I. Lyakh, PhD.

Edited by Matt Thome, M.S. CSCS

Published by:

Ultimate Athlete Concepts

Michigan, USA

2019

For information or to order copies: www.uaconcepts.com

Issurin, Vladimir P.

Lyakh, Vladimir I.

Coordination Abilities of youth and adult athletes

Includes Bibliographical References.

ISBN: 9781796310832

Copyright © 2019 Ultimate Athlete Concepts

All rights reserved – especially the right to copy and distribute. No part of this work may be reproduced – including the photocopy, microfilm or any other means – processed , stored electronically, copied or distributed in any form whatsoever without the express written permission of the publisher.

Printed in the United States of America

Ultimate Athlete Concepts

Website: www.uaconcepts.com

Contents

Preface

Modern civilization dictates insistent and increasing demands to the manifestation of coordination abilities (CA) that embrace all spheres of human activities. The routine life in contemporary, urbanized environments requires permanent execution of a multitude of coordinated movement actions associated with various modes of transportation, human interactions, manipulations with everyday devices, etc. The other branch of CA applications relates to the huge abundance of professional operations performed by various specialists such as drivers, pilots, surgeons, etc., who should execute precise, timely, and organized, highly coordinated actions. But the most salient area of CA manifestation and dominance is in Sport and Physical Education, where coordinative prerequisites largely determine the success or failure of each single movement element of an exercise, match, fight, or race.

For many years, the CA of athletes have held the attention and focus of experts, practitioners and athletes. Their efforts have been directed toward a better understanding of the essence, determining factors, particularities of manifestation, and interaction with other components of athletic mastery such as fitness, physiological and psychological prerequisites, and realization in different sport-specific conditions. During the latest decades, extensive efforts have been directed toward elaboration and verification of the most informative trials and tests that allow for enhanced monitoring of athletes' preparation and characterization of their hidden reserves in coordinative and techno-tactical spheres. In addition, many practically oriented researchers and prominent coaches have persistently searched and elaborated goal-oriented training means that increase the effectiveness of coordination preparation, facilitate acquisition of new sensory motor skills, and positively affect the general progression of athletes.

It is worth noting that the general situation with CA of athletes and their coordination training strikingly differs from the state of knowledge in other branches of sport science and theory of training. Unlike strength, endurance, speed and mental training, where a multitude of extensive books have been published, the coordination aspects of athletic preparation that have been introduced and considered for professional audiences are very scarce. Furthermore, scientific investigations of athletic CA have mostly been fulfilled in Eastern European countries where a number of appropriate books have been published (for instance, the monographs of Meinel and Schnabel, 1988; Mekota and Novosad, 2005; Lyakh, 2006). However, outcomes of these studies and evidence from published books remain restrictedly available for the Western professional audience. At the same time, the interest in athletic CA continues to increase. A number of extensive reviews have been published in peer-reviewed journals devoted to body balance (Zech et al., 2006; Hrysomallis, 2011), kinaesthesia (Proske and Gandevia, 2009) and agility (Sheppard and Young, 2006; Paul et al., 2016). Moreover, contemporary studies of brain activity and neural determinants of movements have largely increased our knowledge concerning physiological prerequisites of highly coordinated movements. A large volume of relevant information has now accumulated in the available literature. In addition, the prominent practice of athletes' preparation provides many examples and experiences of successful implementation of original approaches and training means for purposeful development of various CA and their integration within prospective and efficient training programs. Accessibility of this voluminous material and the anticipated, vivid interest of the professional audience predetermined the decision of the authors to write a new book that will clarify disputable issues concerning the nature and essence of athletic CA. Moreover, the selections of goal-oriented coordination exercises presented in this book should enrich the training repertoire of coaches and athletes for their purposeful coordination programs.

The book's content is comprised of two parts. The first one introduces basic concepts of coordination of athletic movements, including its general consideration, contemporary theory of multilevel construction of highly coordinated motor skills, and a detailed description of basic CA that form the background for attainment of pure techno-tactical mastery in any sport or athletic discipline. The second part introduces practical tools for the evaluation of different CA and descriptions of typical exercises that can be implemented into training programs for purposeful enhancement of coordination potential of youth and high-performance athletes. It is worth noting that general coordination training has one more additional function: it provides valuable input into the prevention of injuries; this benefit cannot be underestimated.

The authors are aware that the exercises described do not satisfy the demands of specialized techno-tactical preparation in several sports. This sport-specific information can be found in appropriate books and manuals. Nevertheless, general coordination training should be considered a valuable resource for the compilation of rationally balanced programs in the preparation of low, medium, and high-level athletes. In addition, a clear understanding of the essence of CA can largely contribute to professional competence of students, scholars, and creative coaches.

Acknowledgements

This book summarizes the extensive efforts of the authors in collection, investigation and elucidation of various items related to the phenomenon of Coordination Abilities of athletes. Working in this direction, we passed long periods in close cooperation with prominent coaches from different countries. Of course, we are very grateful to this professional audience for their fruitful collaboration and vivid interest in the practical aspects of coordination training.

In writing this book we have considered various aspects of coordination training with our colleagues and friends. Psychological aspects of this problem have been considered with Dr. Boris Blumenstein (Israel), who deserves our sincere gratitude and high appreciation.

This book is released by the publishing company "Ultimate Athlete Concepts" and we cordially thank Mr. Yosef Johnson, president of the company, for his valuable support and highly professional collaboration. We also would like to express our gratitude to Mr. Matthew Thome, who edited the text of this book.

In conclusion, we are pleased to thank the readers of our book and hope that its content will assist them in their work and meet their professional expectations.

Part 1

Methodological and scientific background of Coordination Abilities of athletes

The first part of this book is devoted to the introduction of basic knowledge related to the scientific background of CA of athletes. It specifically focuses on the multilevel construction of human movements, acquisition, and construction of motor skills, and the characterization of basic CA from the viewpoint of their essence and manifestation. Special attention is given to hereditary and environmental factors and methodological aspects of purposeful coordination training.

Chapter 1 - Scientific background of movement coordination of athletes

This chapter summarizes basic knowledge and evidence related to movement coordination of athletic performance. Adoption of these general concepts and basic positions form the prerequisites for a better understanding of the essence and resources of coordination training and attainment of technical mastery in different sport activities and athletic disciplines.

1.1 Multi-Level Construction of Human Movements

Coordination is generally described as the control of temporal, spatial, and force variables during the execution of goal-oriented movements or complex motor tasks. The world recognized experts in sports medicine, Hollmann and Hettinger (1990), proposed the definition of movement coordination as "cooperation of the central nervous system and skeletal muscles within some aimed movement process."

For many years, movement coordination has been one of the most disputable matters in sport science. A few decades ago, particularly in Eastern European countries, the commonly accepted movement concept was based on the theory of conditioned reflexes. The founder of this theory, the Nobel Prize Winner Ivan P. Pavlov of Russia, postulated that conditioned reflexes are formed as a response of the Central Nervous System (CNS) to concurrent excitation of a number of neural centers. Following this theory, the formation of a distinct coordination pattern is predisposed by the excitation of appropriate neural centers through muscle receptors, vision, hearing, etc. during the execution of a movement. After a number of repetitions, this pattern becomes consolidated and forms the so-called "dynamic stereotype." The concept of the dynamic stereotype was proposed by Pavlov in 1927 and, for a number of decades, dominated the explanation of the acquisition and refinement of elementary and complex motor skills.

Although the concept of the dynamic stereotype was supported by the authority of great scientists, its limitations were reasonably noticeable in later publications. An alternative concept of movement coordination was proposed by another prominent Soviet physiologist, Nikolai A. Bernstein, who elaborated the original theory of movement coordination and regulation (Figures 1 and 2).

Figure 1. Nikolai A. Bernstein – founder of the contemporary multilevel hierarchical theory of movement coordination

Nikolai A. Bernstein (USSR) is a world-recognized pioneer of research in the area of motor control and motor learning. Using original, precise research methods, he studied various voluntary movement actions and athletic locomotion. Based on abundant objective data, he succeeded in discovering how the Central Nervous System (CNS) is capable of controlling the construction, acquisition, and perfection of motor skills. The scientific legacy of Nikolai A. Bernstein has great value both for the theory and practice of contemporary sport.

The central premise of Professor Bernstein's motor control theory is the fulfillment of movement regulation following a circle-shaped, closed cycle that embraces: the brain – efferent nerves – proprioceptors – muscles – afferent nerves – the brain. The principal moment of this circle is the availability of feedback that the brain receives from muscles, joints, vision, tactile receptors, etc. Following this concept, motor control is based on two circles: internal and external.

The external circle includes feedback from optic, acoustic, vestibular and tactile receptors and is immediately associated with conscious apprehension (Figure 2). This information is immediately predetermined by the movements' variables and environmental factors.

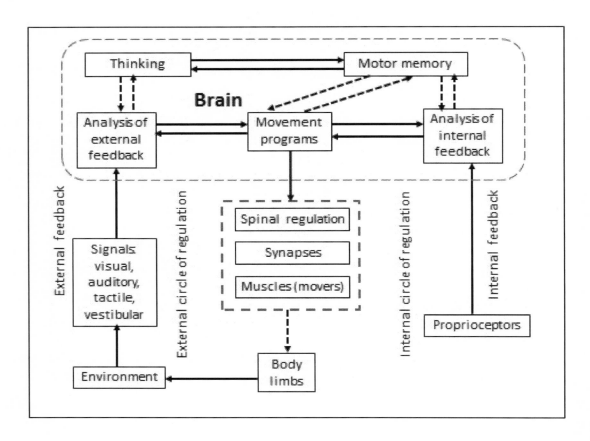

Figure 2. The principal scheme of movement coordination following external and internal circle-shape cycles of regulation (based on Bernstein, 1967 and Chkhaidze, 1968)

The internal circle includes proprioceptive signals from muscles, tendons and joint receptors that come to the brain for analysis. The movements themselves are controlled by appropriate programs that receive internal and external feedback and produce purposeful corrections of coordination patterns. According to Bernstein's concept, movement programs include a model of the targeted action; the real performance is compared with the model and the brain produces sensory corrections for obtaining better correspondence with the model. It is worth noting that during the initial acquisition of a new motor skill, the external circle of movement regulation has prevalent importance and visual, auditory and tactile cues have particular importance. After the initial acquisition of a new motor skill and the formation of the model of the targeted action, contribution of the internal circle of movement regulation largely increases and this leads to automatization of the coordination structure of the movements. From this moment, the central nervous system fulfills the general control of motor performance.

When characterizing human movements, we should emphasize their diversity and complexity, which are predetermined by an abundance of degrees of freedom (DOF) of various body links. In fact, each joint has its own number of DOF that are connected with possible linear and angular displacements of appropriate links. Correspondingly, the total number of DOF of the human body is huge. According to Bernstein, rational movement coordination presupposes reasonable elimination of redundant DOF and involvement of available DOF to produce an optimal strategy of motor control.

It is worth noting that contemporary theory of motor control proposes differentiation between open and closed motor skills. Open skills are characterized by high variability and unpredictability of environmental conditions. This category embraces all ball games such as soccer, tennis, etc., and combat sports like judo, wrestling, etc. Closed skills are realized in situations when environmental conditions are predictable and an athlete's response can be pre-planned. This category includes such sports as gymnastics, track and field disciplines, endurance sports, etc. Correspondingly, coordination demands of these two categories are very different and presuppose employment of appropriate training approaches for each sport-specific situation.

Further sections of this book introduce more voluminous and detailed information on movement coordination and coordination abilities that have distinct importance for advanced preparation of high-performance and amateur athletes.

A better understanding of movement coordination presupposes acquaintance with the principal positions of a movement's construction that were proposed in the classic theory of N.A. Bernstein and remain important for both scholars and practitioners. Let us consider the four principal levels of a movement's construction.

1.1.1. Level of Tone

This level presupposes maintenance of a natural tone of postural muscles, namely the body and neck, which provides a background for all daily activities and execution of every athletic exercise. These permanent muscular efforts counteract any disturbances of balance during athletic activities and forces produced by loaded, upper-body actions. Muscular tone activities are characterized by the prevalence of smooth, elastic and fatigue resistant contractions. The background function of tonic, muscular exertion is extremely important for performance of all cyclic and acyclic locomotor action. Importantly, tonic contractions of body muscles usually do not require special voluntary control. However, in several athletic disciplines, appropriate cues for regulation of postural behavior are necessary and commonly accepted; For example, in gymnastics, diving, ski jumping, etc. In addition, the background activity of tonic muscles may increase irritability and readiness for excitation of spinal neurons and therefore affect performance of other voluntary actions.

Of course, the level of tone has no leading position in the movement hierarchy, but its background function provides the foundation for all upper levels and, as Bernstein noted, can be named the "background of backgrounds." Moreover, the additional function of voluntary relaxation of tonic muscles has proper importance in various psychological techniques such as counteraction to emotional stress.

1.1.2. Level of Synergies

This level was historically developed for proper fulfillment of locomotor activities. In fact, muscle synergy serves for the specific activation of movement patterns involving appropriate sets of muscles and muscular-articular linkages to produce a purposeful movement. The biggest adva1.1.2 ntage of this level is its ability to control basic, voluminous locomotion such as walking, running, etc. In addition, it serves as a background for execution of more local actions demanding high precision and accuracy. The supreme center of regulation of activity at this level is located in a sub-cortical area of the brain termed the *dorsal pallidum*, but transition of any kind of sensory signal is fulfilled with the help of another part of the brain called the *thalamus*. Thanks to the close connection of this level with the thalamus, as the center of reception activity, it produces the majority of sensory corrections, which are important contributors in the formation of highly coordinated motor skills. In addition, the level of synergies provides proper control of the rhythmic structure of movements and interaction of a muscle's antagonists. This level of regulation also provides accurate reproduction of subsequent movements in cyclic locomotion. This characteristic is closely connected with the formation of new motor skills and their automatization. However, such movement regulation has distinct limitations; It is poorly connected with visual and acoustic receptors. Thus, this level succeeds in providing internal regulation of synergy but does not succeed to provide its rational interaction with environmental conditions. Notably, as with the level of basic backgrounds, this level fulfills the accumulation of various locomotor experiences and this storage is effectively exploited during the formation of new, unknown and non-accustomed motor skills.

Of course, this level of movement construction still does not serve for formation of highly coordinated athletic skills, but it accumulates a large setting of motor backgrounds that are utilized for creation of more specialized, purposeful movement patterns within the upper "level of Space" and supreme "level of Action."

1.1.3. Level of Space

This level of movements' construction encompasses a large group of activities associated with goal-directed displacements of the body and several body limbs in space. On one hand, it demands the ability to clearly perceive spatial dimensions of several objects and distances between them and objective judgment of angular and linear displacements of body limbs. On the other hand, it presupposes the ability to recognize various movement shapes and reproduce them with sufficient accuracy and reliability. The movements representing this level include goal-directed transference of the body and its limbs when changing position and spatial orientation. The majority of such movements are short-term and acyclic. The list of typical movements from this level includes various jumps, throws and technical elements from artistic and rhythmic gymnastics. This group also includes athletic locomotion with various devices such as skis, skates, rollers, a bicycle, etc. In addition, the large spectrum of resisted drills, including any kind of free-weight exercises, are also part of these settings. Notably, the execution of the mentioned elements and exercises demand high accuracy, which can be provided by appropriate mechanisms of neural regulation, enabling their level of space. The neural center responsible for the regulation of the mentioned movements is the *striatum*, which is located in the subcortical part of the brain.

Importantly, the movements representing this level actively involve motor backgrounds from the previous level of synergy. Purposeful utilization of sensory corrections largely assists in achievement of desirable accuracy and reliability of spatial exercises.

1.1.4. Level of Action

This level fulfills the supreme control of movements and is reasonably termed the "highest level." Following the expression of Bernstein, it is "properly, the human level" because of its firm association with conscious planning and execution of meaningful actions. Notably, as a rule, motor action is not single movement; It includes a chain of sequenced movements, which are the links of a chain and elements of an entire action. Its principal particularity is purposefulness. Following descending command from the premotor cortex of the brain, the muscles fulfill appropriate, goal-oriented action using necessary movement-links. Frequent performance of certain actions leads to their automatization and the creation of background coordination that is utilized in several motor skills. These motor skills replace more primitive movements produced within the previously considered levels of space and synergies. These more or less automatized actions are based on motor memory and conscious planning of meaningful motor behavior. Moreover, these actions actively exploit various leading corrections that determine achievement of the planned result. Thus, the sources of leading corrections are true notions of the planned result of action.

Importantly, the level of Action fulfills permanent control of all movement-links and their chains, providing their purposeful functioning. The principal particularity of such construction is the utilization of movement elements that were produced at the lower levels of Space and Synergies. However, these movement elements were elaborated not occasionally, but following desires and demands from the supreme level of Action. Therefore, the linkage of movement elements and their functioning occurs under continuous control of appropriate brain structures and is associated with the conscious comprehension of the athlete. Unlike the lower levels of movements' construction, the supreme level of Action produces precise motor skills that form the content of techno-tactical mastery in combat sports, ball games, gymnastics, track and field, etc.

The main functions and important particularities of the above listed levels of the motor control system are summarized below (Table 1).

Table 1. Characterization of the levels of movement construction, their main functions and particularities (based on Bernstein, 1947 and 1967)

Levels of movement construction	Main functions	Comments
Level of Tone	Regulation of muscular tone and control of the excitability of spinal structures	This level provides background function for all upper levels
Level of Synergies	Control of specific activation of movement patterns of basic locomotion such as walking, running, etc.	Additional function is the control of the rhythmic structure of movements and interaction of muscles-antagonists.
Level of Space	Control of goal-directed displacements of the body and several body limbs in space	These movements are mostly short-term and acyclic such as jumps, throws, resisted drills, etc.
Level of Action	Compilation and control of purposeful motor action consisting of many elements	This process is associated with voluntary control and conscious comprehension of the athlete

It is worth noting that the centers of motor regulation of the right side of the human body are usually located in the left hemisphere of brain. Correspondingly, in a major part of the population, the right arm is more precise and stronger than the left arm. A smaller portion of humans are left hand/arm dominant and the location of motor regulation is in the right hemisphere. Among the representatives of this sub-population, we can find exceptionally talented athletes in tennis, boxing, throws, etc. The reasons for such exclusiveness are unclear, but this phenomenon of left-handedness raises continuous interest of both scientists and coaches.

1.2 Acquisition and construction of motor skills

Motor skills form the basis and content of techno-tactical mastery in any sport. Their physiological nature provides them with large variability, reliability and stability in different conditions. According to Bernstein's definition, motor skill should be considered the acquired ability to solve an appropriate motor task and obtain the desired goal of the movement. The central nervous system of an individual constructs a motor skill following his conscious demand and this complex process consists of a number of successive stages. During this process, an athlete fulfills the initial acquisition of a skill, formation of a rough structure of the movement, and the final acquirement of the motor skill. The entire process of motor skill construction occurs using various background corrections and thorough control from the supreme level of movement regulation, i.e. the level of Action. Let's now consider all stages of motor skill construction.

The first stage is familiarization with the new skill and its movement's content. A motor skill itself is not a homogenous action; it contains a leading element and auxiliary links. Usually familiarization is started from demonstration of movement and its explanation from the coach. Afterwards, an athlete executes several attempts to reproduce the movement, focusing on its leading element. In the beginning, movement regulation occurs from the level of Action and requires conscious comprehension and control from an athlete. However, step-by-step, the central nervous system begins to involve background corrections from the level of Synergies and the level of Space. From there, an athlete can control some auxiliary links of the skill automatically and concentrate on the leading element. After a number of repetitions, the athlete acquires the principal structure of the new skill and begins to refine it, focusing on reliable execution and its adjustment for unique particularities of the individual.

The second stage is devoted to the skill's enhancement and its essence is mobilization and utilization of sensory-motor corrections. Unlike the previous stage, an athlete is not focused on an external image of the movement, but on internal perception and comprehension of proprioceptive signals. The reasonable response from the central nervous system is descending and accumulation of appropriate sensory-motor corrections that allow for correction of several movement errors and improvement of general motor coordination. This stage requires multiple executions of the motor skill and accumulation of very useful experience. As a result, the central nervous system selects the most efficient sensory-motor corrections for subsequent employment in practice. A conscious attitude toward exercising and attention to its details allow for the process of motor learning and construction of rational skill to be largely accelerated.

The third stage presupposes automatization of the motor skill. Multiple repetitions of a certain skill are associated with the involvement of background corrections and motor control shifts, partly to lower level movement regulation such as the level of Synergies and the level of Space. This shift leads to liberation of the supreme level of Action from continuous motor control and movement can be performed without conscious supervision of an individual; Therefore, the movement can be performed automatically. These motor automatisms may be even more flexible and adaptable than consciously executed movements. For instance, in the initial stage of learning, an athlete controls many details of cycling or swimming motions. Movement automatization leads to more reliable and skilled performance when an athlete should control the most meaningful elements of the movement and behavioral responses. In ball games and combat sports, such automatization allows an athlete to increase concentration on tactical components of performance.

The last stage of motor skill construction is movement stabilization. When the motor skill is sufficiently automatized the movement can be reproduced accurately many times. Thus, this skill has reached high stability. However, imagine a situation when the external conditions of performance are changed. May some interference such as insufficient lighting, cold temperatures, or holes in playing the surface affect some skill execution? Definitely – yes. Therefore, the skill should be resistant to any kind of disturbances. This ability to adapt movement to different external conditions is provided with involvement of urgent sensory-motor corrections and automatic regulation of motor behavior. In this case, an athlete should control the general situation whereas the autonomic automatisms of movement regulation provide appropriate adjustment of the skill to the changed conditions. These increased demands to motor skill stabilization are typical for various outdoor sports such as rowing, canoeing, skiing, etc. However, routine practice in ball games and combat sports is firmly associated with interactions with opponents and various technical skills should be performed against active counteraction of rivals.

Another type of interference is associated with internal causes of aggravating performance of motor skills. These interferences include fatigue, emotional tension, impact of previous injuries, etc. Of course, trained athletes demonstrate a high level of fatigue tolerance and emotional control. Apparently the ability to maintain efficient skill performance despite fatigue, emotional tension and neuromuscular disorders presupposes a high level of motor skill stabilization and forms a specific component of techno-tactical mastery.

Concluding this section, it is worth noting that automatization and stabilization of motor skills allow the athlete to be concentrated on the most important, meaningful demands of his/her athletic activity. Usually these demands are firmly associated with the tactical particularities of the current performance. Correspondingly, particularly in ball games and combat sports, the term "techno-tactical skill" is widely used, referring to the motor skill's close association with general tasks of some match or fight.

Chapter 2 - Athletic Coordination Abilities: essence and manifestation

Coordinative Abilities (CA) are reasonably considered an indispensable component of the motor potential of athletes, which largely affect athletic performances and attainment of sport excellence. Although the importance of CA is widely recognized, the general situation with their interpretation is paradoxical. On one hand, CA are mentioned and described in all textbooks of theory of training and exercise physiology. On the other hand, their descriptions in different sources are equivocal, not sufficiently systematized, and frequently contain erroneous positions. For instance, several analysts have specified and considered five basic CA (Hirtz, 1985; Mekota, 2000), whereas the others have highlighted six (Schnabel,2001), seven, and more coordination components (Starosta, 2006; Simonek, 2014). Various aspects of CA trainability remain disputable and require clarification.

2.1. Classification of basic CA of athletes

Experimental studies of CA were traditionally popular in Eastern European countries and, therefore, their outcomes were restrictedly available for the worldwide professional audience. Nevertheless, during recent decades, a large number of publications have been released. The purpose of this section is to introduce the most relevant outcomes of the published studies and positions of analysts from different countries and various sports.

As it was previously stated, there are a number of versions of basic CA classifications introduced by different analysts. One of the most widely used and commonly accepted versions proposes a classification that includes basic CA components, namely: kinesthetic differentiation, rhythmic ability, spatial orientation, complex motor reaction, and balance ability (Hirtz, 1985; Mekota, 2000). A number of later publications have also verified agility as an important component of basic CA (Sheppard and Young, 2006; Paul et al., 2016). Thus, we will operate with the six basic CA that have received the most popularity and general acceptance in the professional community. Their definitions and relevant particularities are presented below (Table 2).

Table 2. Classification and definitions of basic CA of athletes

Basic CA	Definitions	Comments
Kinaesthetic differentiation	Ability to differentiate spatial, temporal and strength characteristics of movement in accordance to given conditions	This ability is affected by sensory input from various receptors
Rhythmic ability	Ability to notice, memorize, adjust and reproduce temporal rhythm and movement rates of motor performance	This ability is realized both in cyclic and acyclic motor performances
Spatial orientation	Ability to determine and adequately regulate body position and motor behavior in space	This ability is a prerequisite for proper performance of spatial motor tasks
Complex motor reaction	Ability to react accurately and rapidly to stimuli that must be recognized from among other signals	Outcomes of complex motor reactions are associated with decision-making processes
Agility	Ability to rapidly change movement direction and react to pre-planned or sudden stimuli	There are 2 modes: "planned agility" and "reactive agility"
Balance ability	Ability to control spatial body position while maintaining its equilibrium and postural stability	Static and dynamic balance ability should be distinguished

It should be noted that basic CA form the general background for each sport activity. In addition, there are a multitude of sport-specific CA that are closely associated with appropriate motor skills and technical demands. Perceptual-cognitive adaptations produced by sport-specific training determine the development of specialized "sense of the water," "feel for the ball," etc. that largely affect coordination patterns of technical performances in appropriate sports. Nevertheless, a general background of basic CA is equally important for all sports and athletic disciplines. Let's consider the above listed CA properly.

2.2. Kinaesthetic differentiation

Manifestation of this CA presupposes the perception of sensory input produced by various receptors during the movement and subsequent differentiation of spatial, temporal and strength characteristics of motor performance. This ability has principal importance for conscious regulation of the movement pattern and muscular efforts. Regulation of spatial characteristics concerns amplitude, direction and velocity of movement; muscular efforts and force application in isometric and dynamic conditions are regulated as well. Acquisition of new technical skills in any sport is closely associated with the ability to differentiate limb position, movement length, speed, and force application. In highly coordinative, esthetic sports, such as gymnastics, figure skating, synchronized swimming, etc. this ability can play a crucial role in the attainment of athletic mastery and virtuosity of performance.

One of the classic examples of pronounced manifestation of kinesthetic differentiation is associated with Olympic archery, where demands to regulation of spatial, force and temporal characteristics immediately affect the outcomes of athletic performance (Figure 3).

Figure 3. Archery performance of Olympic Champion Ku Bon-chan of South Korea who won two gold medals in team and individual events at the 2016 Summer Olympics in Rio de Janeiro

The testing protocol for kinaesthetic differentiation presupposes the evaluation of accuracy and repeatability of various motor performances. Findings of several studies illustrate research approaches and the contribution of kinaesthetic differentiation to the technical motor potential of athletes representing different sports (Table 3).

Table 3. Summary of studies evaluating kinaesthetic differentiation of athletes

Study	Test description	Study outcomes
Lech et al., 2011	Computerized test using the Toshiba Satellite R15 program adapted for judo fighting	Fight activity of trained judokas is highly correlated with their movement differentiation ability
Pakosz, 2012	Shooting basketballs using balls of different weights and size	More competent players showed higher precision, lower variability and lower EMG values during the shots
Rejman et al., 2012	Examination of forces that act on a monofin during swimming stroke and simulation trials in dry-land conditions	The repeatability of force application in water conditions was much higher compared to repetition accuracy during simulation trials in dry-land conditions
Bańkosz, 2012	Assessment of angular accuracy in forearm pronation/supination in table tennis players	In all tests more skilled players manifested greater movement accuracy and lower variability of angular displacements
Rana and Rajpoot, 2015	Backward medicine ball throw with estimation of accuracy in distance repeatability	Kinaesthetic differentiation ability had high importance for technical skill in table tennis and a lower impact on badminton skill
Mustafa et al., 2015	Assessment of isometric dominant and non-dominant hand gripping with 100%, 50% and 25% of maximal effort	Application of 9 min of Swedish massage doesn't affect kinesthetic differentiation and maximal force application in isometric hand gripping

The outcomes of the reviewed studies provide evidence that the ability of kinaesthetic differentiation largely affects fight activity of trained judokas (Lech et al., 2011), precision and repeatability of basketball shots (Pakosz, 2012), repeatability of force application to a monofin during underwater swimming (Rejman et al., 2012) and technical mastery of table tennis players (Bańkosz, 2012; Rana and Rajpoot, 2015). It was also revealed that this ability is sufficiently resistant to external factors acting on the muscles such as Swedish massage (Mustafa et al, 2015).

From a physiological viewpoint, kinaesthetic differentiation is based on proprioceptive signals produced from two sources: the sense of position and the sense of movement (Proske, 2006). It is commonly accepted that muscle spindles are primarily responsible for both the sense of movement and the sense of position. However, the processing of signals related to movement and/or position is done by separate mechanisms. Investigations of neuronal discharges in the primary motor cortex have revealed neurons that transmit appropriate signals during postural tasks and others that activate exclusively during movement tasks (Kurtzer et al., 2006). Sensory signals contributing to kinaesthetic differentiation descend from three sources: tactile, visual and proprioceptive analyzers. Findings of neuroimaging studies have provided evidence that the brain permanently matches visual and proprioceptive inputs, providing the linkage between what the athlete feels and what they see. Thus, kinaesthetic differentiation is based on the integration of all sensory inputs in brain.

2.3. Rhythmic ability

Rhythm of movement is an essential characteristic of motor performance in any sport. Correspondingly, rhythmic ability is an indispensable property that largely determines an athlete's performance in both training routines and competitions. Manifestation of this ability is realized in two modes: as the ability to reproduce a given predetermined movement rate in cyclic exercises (1), and as the ability to reproduce a specially structured movement rhythm in acyclic motor tasks (2). The first mode can be illustrated by the maintenance of a race-pace pattern during running, swimming, skating, etc. The second mode is realized in various jumping and throwing performances, technical elements from ball games and combat sports, as well as performance of any stunts in gymnastics. Rhythmic ability has crucial importance for successful performance in esthetic sports such as figure skating, rhythmic gymnastics and athletic dances. Rhythmic gymnastics can be viewed as a very representative area of accentuated manifestation of rhythmic ability (Figure 4).

Figure 4. Margarita Mamun (Russia) – Olympic Champion in rhythmic gymnastics at the 2016 Summer Olympics in Rio de Janeiro

Example of outstanding athlete. Margarita Mamun started her gymnastics activity at age 7; at the age of 10 she started her purposeful, professional preparation in rhythmic gymnastics. She was born in Moscow; her mother was a former gymnast, father was citizen of Bangladesh. Thus, Margarita had both Russian and Bangladesh citizenship. At age 16 she earned 4 gold medals in the senior Russian Championship. At age 18, 19 and 20 Margarita won 7 gold medals at the World Championships in different disciplines (ball, clubs, ribbon and hoop). In the Rio de Janeiro Olympics, Margarita earned the gold medal in all-around score and achieved a new Olympic Record under the 20 point judging system.

Rhythmic ability was extensively studied with regards to the initial preparation and motor learning of children, fitness training of recreational athletes, acquisition of sport-specific technical skills, and advanced preparation of high-performance athletes (Table 4).

Studies of young athletes revealed their significant superiority in rhythmic ability compared to the non-athletic control group. Apparently, regular training in tennis provides substantial stimulation of coordination abilities including sense of rhythm (Zachopoulou et al.,2000). Furthermore, improved ability of rhythm reproduction positively affects language performance in children of 4-8 years of age (Haines, 2003). The research findings have shown that motor activities accompanied by music produce a beneficial impact on rhythmic ability of pre-school children compared to other training forms (Agdiniotis et al., 2009). Interestingly, girls attained superior rhythmic performance when compared to boys. A high contribution of rhythmic ability to the acquisition of a new motor skill was revealed in a study with novice alpine skiers; the individuals with higher rhythmic potential were more successful in motor learning (Oreb et al., 2011).

Table 4. Summary of studies examining rhythmic abilities

Study	Study design	Study outcomes
Zachopoulou et al.,2000	4 groups of children aged 9.2 ± 4.8 years, a total of 203 athletes, from different sports were examined with regard to rhythmic abilities	Tennis players showed higher accuracy than basketball players and swimmers. All athletes obtained better performance at fast vs. slow tempo.
Haines, 2003	Rhythm reproduction and language performance abilities were examined in 1013 children aged 4-8 yrs	Associations were found between rhythm reproduction and language performance in all age groups
Agdiniotis et al., 2009	Rhythmic ability was examined in pre-school children (n=120) engaging in physical activities accompanied or not by music.	Children experienced in motor activities accompanied by music showed the best rhythmic performance. Girls produced better results than boys
Chałupka et al., 2009	Rhythmic ability of 35 female recreational athletes was examined before and after completion of aqua aerobic training program	Successfulness of rhythm reproduction depends on movement pace and task; running exercises are beneficial compared to jumping performances
Oreb et al., 2011	108 novice alpine skiers completed tests of rhythm reproduction combined with acquisition of ski-specific skills	Rhythm reproduction largely affects acquisition of basic alpine skiing skills. Better rhythmic coordination produces more efficient motor learning
Sögüt et al., 2012	30 trained tennis players completed 3 program versions: general rhythm training, tennis-specific rhythm training, control tennis group	Tennis specific rhythm training provided superior enhancement of both tennis competence and rhythmic ability of players
Sögüt & Kirazci, 2014	Rhythmic ability of 32 young trained tennis players and 32 inactive control persons was examined with paces of 50 and 120 beats per minute	Tennis players showed significant superiority in rhythm reproduction compared to non-athletes. No gender effect was noted
Sommer et al., 2014	13 trained male golfers underwent a 4-week program of synchronized metronome training (SMT) to enhance the rhythmic structure of golf-swing performance	SMT resulted in increased golf-shot accuracy and enhanced reproduction of motor skill. It is suggested that improved brain-based control was induced by specialized rhythmic training

It was established that rhythmic ability of adult recreational female athletes can be substantially improved following an aqua aerobic fitness program that includes a large amount of rhythmic exercises (Chałupka et al., 2009). It can be suggested that motor tasks with rhythm reproduction should be incorporated into the fitness training of recreational athletes.

Special interest is drawn from studies devoted to the implementation of "Rhythm training" in the preparation of qualified athletes. The effect of generalized and specialized programs of rhythmic exercises was evaluated during the preparation of trained tennis players (Sögüt et al., 2012 and 2014). The program of general rhythm training included execution of various motor tasks: side, front and back jumps, hand clapping, walking in place at a slow or fast tempo, etc. A tennis-specific rhythm training program encompassed various combinations of bouncing tennis balls with and without a racket in place and while walking at a slow or fast tempo. Study outcomes have shown that tennis specific rhythm exercises evoked preferable enhancement of technical mastery and rhythmic ability of athletes, whereas the control tennis program positively affected the sport-specific competence but not the rhythmic potential of the players.

A similar study was realized during the preparation of trained golf players, who practiced synchronized metronome rhythm training (Sommer et al., 2014). The program included executions of hand clapping and tapping one or two legs on a footpad at various paces with rhythmical, auditory cues. The four week intervention program resulted in significant improvement of the biomechanical structure of the golf swing and an increased reproducibility of temporal-spatial characteristics during serial swing performance.

The physiological background of rhythmic ability of athletes is derived from abundant data of recent studies using neuroimaging techniques. It is known that rhythmically organized motor tasks activate subcortical and cortical brain areas. Individual differences in rhythm perception were revealed when comparing the brain activity of individuals who successfully perceive an implied rhythm with those who do not (Yarrow et al, 2009). Correspondingly, the motor behavior of athletes is mediated by the activation of cortical circuits involved in rhythm production. It is known that rhythm perception presupposes both automatic and cognitively controlled regulation. The recent studies emphasize the role of the cerebellum in perception and acquisition of rhythmic stimulation. It is suggested that the cerebellum contributes to motor coordination, precise motor timing and temporal precision of voluntary motor actions (Ivry and

Schlerf, 2008). Importantly, feedback signals largely contribute to maintenance of the rhythmical organization of movement. It is also notable that variability in rhythmically paced tapping substantially decreases in cases when the motor task is accompanied by systematic feedback (Wing et al., 2010).

2.4. Spatial orientation

Spatial orientation has a broad spectrum of applications including judgment and regulation of body position, assessment of location of partners and opponents in ball games, determination of rational motor behavior following external conditions, evaluation and regulation of spatial movement patterns in any sport, judgment of location and spatial displacements of an opponent in combat sports, etc. (Stølen et al., 2005; Monteiro et al., 2010). This ability is closely associated with cognitive skills that provide an adequate motor response following available spatial information. Of course, manifestation of this ability is sport-specific and has particular importance in artistic and rhythmic gymnastics, ball games and combat sports where demands of spatial ability are very pronounced.

Figure 5. Simone Biles (USA) – legendary artistic gymnast. This picture can serve as extremely impressive example of the exclusive demands to spatial orientation in contemporary world sport

Example of an outstanding athlete. Simone Biles started her athletic activity in gymnastics at age 6 and began purposeful preparation in artistic gymnastics at age 8. She began her competition career at age 14 and placed 5th in the balance beam and floor exercise in the junior Illinois competition. At age 15, Simone joined the US Junior National team. However, at age 16 she won two gold medals in the senior World Championship in the all-around program and floor exercise. At ages 17 and 18 she won 8 gold medals at the World Championships as a US team member, in the all-around program, balance beam and floor exercise. At the Olympic Games in Rio de Janeiro, Simone Biles earned 4 gold medals: as a US team member, all-around, vault, and floor exercise, in addition to a bronze medal in the balance beam.

Evaluation of spatial orientation in athletes presupposes the determination of accuracy and speed of performances of specially designed motor tasks.

Spatial abilities of the human population and spatial orientation of athletes were extensively studied with regards to various aspects of their manifestation and improvement. Mental rotation, as one of the most illustrative modes of spatial ability, has drawn the particular attention of researchers (Table 5). Mental rotation can be characterized as the ability to mentally transform two and three-dimensional objects in order to imagine how they look from different points of view (Jansen and Lehmann, 2013).

Table 5. Summary of studies examining spatial orientation

Study	Study design	Study outcomes
Lord and Garrison, 1998	Spatial ability of 150 female and 150 male collegiate athletes representing different sports was examined using the mental rotation test	No gender difference was found in baseball, swimming and track and field. Female basketball players showed significant superiority compared to male players
Moreau et al., 2012	Changes of spatial abilities of 62 athletes following 10 months of wrestling (n=31) or running (n=31) training were evaluated using the mental rotation test	Wrestling group achieved significantly higher enhancement of spatial ability compared to running group. Male athletes outperformed females both in the pretest and the posttest trials
Hijazi, 2013	8 female and 8 male qualified fencers were examined with regard to their visual-spatial abilities and level of athletic competence	Significant and high correlations were revealed between characteristics of visual-spatial abilities and level of athletic achievements in both genders
Jansen and Lehmann, 2013	Spatial ability of qualified athletes (40 gymnasts, 40 soccer players) and 40 non-athletes was examined using the mental rotation test with cubic and human figures	The gymnasts but not soccer players showed superior spatial ability compared to non-athletes. Male athletes obtained higher scores of mental rotation than females
Notarnicola et al., 2014	Junior female and male volleyball (n=60), tennis players (n=60), non-athletes (n=60) underwent a blind-folded spatial orientation test moving from and returning to starting point	Volleyball and tennis players showed significant superiority compared to non-athletes with no difference between boys and girls. In non-athletic group boys significantly outperformed girls
Stoyanova et al. 2016	69 regional or national level female and male athletes from different sports were examined using computerized tests of spatial orientation from the Vienna test system	National level athletes significantly outperformed regional athletes. A significant correlation was found between sport experience and spatial ability. No gender effects were found

A number of studies were devoted to the comparison of spatial ability of athletes with non-athletic volunteers. A study of adolescent volleyball and tennis players revealed their significant superiority compared to non-athletes (Notarnicola et al., 2014). These outcomes are not consistent with findings of another study where a higher level of spatial ability compared with non-athletes was reported in gymnasts but not in soccer players (Jansen and Lehmann, 2013). Two other studies revealed significantly increased spatial ability in national level athletes compared to their lower qualified counterparts (Stoyanova et al. ,2016) and a high correlation between spatial ability and level of athletic achievements (Hijazi, 2013). Apparently, purposeful athletic preparation consistently increases the spatial ability of athletes although the extent of this impact depends on sport-specific demands and particularities of evaluation trials. For instance, training in wrestling, where the demands of spatial orientation are highly accentuated, resulted in a more pronounced enhancement of spatial ability than training in running (Moreau et al., 2012).

Sex differentiation of spatial ability was extensively studied and discussed by many researchers. The widely accepted position claims that males display a higher level of spatial ability than females (Linn M, Petersen, 1985 for review). This supposition is partly supported by findings of another study (Moreau et al., 2012). Nevertheless, a study of qualified swimmers, baseball players and track and field athletes did not find any differences in spatial ability between males and females. Moreover, female basketball players outperformed their male counterparts in a spatial test of mental rotation (Lord and Garrison,1998). Similarly, no gender difference was found in a study of qualified volleyball and tennis players (Notarnicola et al., 2014) and advanced athletes from different sports (Stoyanova et al. 2016). Notably, in the non-athletic population, spatial superiority of males was repeatedly reported (Linn M, Petersen, 1985). Evidentially, purposeful athletic preparation reduces and even eliminates the spatial advantages of males associated with evolutionary and biological prerequisites of this coordinative phenomenon.

Studies of evolutionary prerequisites of spatial ability provide a valuable contribution to the general explanation of gender differences in the non-athletic population. A number of hypotheses were offered to explain the spatial male advantage in an evolutionary context. Following the hypothesis of fertility and parental care, females were forced to reduce mobility during reproductive periods whereas males executed their spatial activities for hunting and warfare (Jones et al., 2003).

The hypothesis of male foraging assumes that ancient men were required to develop and enhance their spatial abilities involved in hunting (Silverman et al., 2000). Following the male warfare hypothesis, ancient men covered long distances, participating in various conflicts with other groups, competing for food resources and capturing females (Buss et al., 1997). One more hypothesis proposes that successful hunters obtained higher social status in ancient populations and increased spatial abilities contributed into the attainment of such status (Sherry and Hampson, 1997). In any case, evolutionary roots allow for a better understanding of the nature of spatial orientation and its importance for the coordinative potential of athletes.

Recent studies of athletes using magnetic resonance imaging (MRI) have revealed increased cortical thickness in brain areas related to visual-spatial control (Wei et al., 2011). It was also revealed that in male athletes, spatial processing is localized in the right hemisphere, whereas female athletes did not show a hemisphere preference (Vogel et al., 2003). The particular role of spatial navigation belongs to a specialized region of the brain called the hippocampus. Its function provides the determination of some individual's location and how to navigate to the next destination (Shrager et al., 2007). The hormonal status of athletes also largely affects the manifestation of spatial orientation. It is known that a lower testosterone level of male athletes is beneficial for spatial abilities, whereas in female athletes, higher testosterone is associated with more favorable spatial orientation (Jones et al., 2003).

2.5. Complex motor reaction

Reaction time is one of the most widely used psychophysiological indicators in sport practice and research. There are two basic kinds of motor reactions:

1. Simple motor reaction: when an athlete responds to one stimulus as soon as possible. The stimulus can be an acoustic or visual signal, the motor action can be pressing a button, spacebar, etc.;
2. Complex motor reaction: when an athlete must recognize the appropriate stimulus among other stimuli and react to it. They are evaluated on accurateness and speed of motor reaction.

Indicators of simple motor reactions characterize general quickness and are widely used for psychophysiological diagnostics of athletes, operators, drivers, pilots, etc., whereas indicators of complex motor reactions purely reflect the coordinative potential of individuals, including the decision-making process of when an adequate reaction should be selected. Correspondingly, simple motor reaction time is much shorter (on average, by 220ms) as compared to complex motor reaction (Kida et al., 2005). In the literature, complex motor reaction is frequently referred to as "choice reaction" and "multiple choice reaction" (Table 6).

The area of application of complex motor reaction is huge, implying, first of all, a multitude of unpredictable situations in ball games and combat sports. The typical scenario presupposes the rapid and efficient reaction following the action of an opponent and/or partner. Such situations constantly occur in tennis, where demands to manifestation of complex motor reactions are particularly high. During the recent decade, World leading tennis player Roger Federer has demonstrated exceptionally high reactivity, which is part of his magnificent athletic talent (Figure 6).

Figure 6. Roger Federer (Switzerland), World leading tennis player who demonstrates excellent complex motor reactions in his competitive and training activities

Example of an outstanding athlete. Roger Federer is one of the most famous tennis players in the World. He started his regular tennis preparation at age 8 and at age 11 he was one of the Top 3 junior players in Switzerland. At age 17, Roger became the winner of junior Wimbledon and, in fact, earned the title of Junior World champion of the year. The awards record of this great athlete includes an Olympic gold medal (2008-doubles), an Olympic silver medal (2012-singles), winning of 17 Grand Slam tournaments and many other prestigious competitions.

Evaluation of complex motor reaction is fulfilled using sport-specific research designs and computerized testing systems. The most widely used tools offer a computerized Vienna test system that allows for the examination of both simple and complex motor reactions (Schuhfriegd, 1996).

Studies of complex motor reactions were conducted with the aim to evaluate the trainability of this CA component and its dependence on administration of various workloads (Table 6).

Table 6. Summary of studies examining complex motor reaction in athletes

Study	Study design	Study outcomes
Williams and Walmsley, 2000	Simple and choice motor reactions of 3 elite and 3 novice fencers were measured using EMG	Elite fencers largely outperformed novices in simple and particularly in choice sport-specific motor tasks
Mori et al., 2002	Choice reaction (CR) of 6 trained and 7 novice karate athletes was measured using videotaped or neutral stimuli	CR after video-clips of offensive actions was longer but superiority of experts compared to novices was much larger than after neutral stimuli
Lemmink and Visscher, 2005	CR was measured in 8 amateur soccer players before and after intermittent aerobic bouts. Control group did not perform any exercises	Reaction speed and accuracy were similarly enhanced in in both groups. Moderate aerobic workloads did not affect CR of soccer players
Guizani et al., 2006	Choice reaction (CR) was measured in 12 professional fencers and 12 non-athletes before and after aerobic pedaling	The fencers but not control subjects showed shorter CR after load equal to 40%, 60% and 80% of maximal aerobic power compared to preload level
Nakamoto and Mori, 2008	CR was measured in 24 baseball, 20 basketball players differing in skill level, and in 13 non-athletic students	Basketball and baseball players had significantly shorter CR than non-athletes. Skilled baseball players had superior CR compared to less experienced players
Ghuntla et al., 2014	Simple and CR of 50 male amateur athletes were measured before and after a workout in which visual-motor responses were trained	A single workout with visual-motor training resulted in significant enhancement of both simple and complex motor reactions of subjects
Frýbort et al., 2016	CR following video-clip of offensive action was measured in 42 elite junior soccer players before and after training loads of different intensities	Moderate intensity exercises didn't reduce CR; high-intensity anaerobic load had a negative effect on CR and accuracy of motor response

The complex motor reaction of fencers and karate athletes compared to novices was evaluated using sport-specific motor tasks and stimuli (Ghuntla et al., 2014; Frýbort et al. 2016). Notably, the sport-specific stimuli appeared to be much more sensitive to competence level compared to neutral stimuli. Similarly, qualified basketball and baseball players have shown superior complex motor reaction compared to less competent counterparts (Nakamoto and Mori, 2008). It was also revealed that moderate training workloads don't impair complex reaction ability in professional fencers (Guizani et al., 2006), adult amateur (Ghuntla et al., 2014) or junior elite soccer players (Frýbort et al. 2016). Contrary to that, training workloads produce a negative impact on motor reaction in non-athletic subjects (Guizani et al., 2006). Interestingly, even a single workout with visual-motor stimulation can produce significant enhancement of both the simple and complex motor reaction of amateur athletes (Ghuntla et al., 2014).

Unlike simple motor reactions that are conditioned by visual-sensory input and properties of the central nervous system, the complex motor reaction largely depends on cognitive factors and the decision-making process. A summary of a number of studies provides evidence that the efficiency of complex choice reaction is firmly associated with three essential determinants of the decision-making process: attention, anticipation, and memory (Afonso et al., 2012). Selective attentional control of expert athletes is focused on specific aspects of motor action, aiming to detect the most relevant indicators. The whole set of available information presupposes the involvement of an anticipation strategy that largely determines the speed and accuracy of a motor response. A study of successful soccer goalkeepers revealed that rational anticipation behavior significantly increases the rate of accuracy and adequacy of their motor reactions (Savelsbergh et al., 2005). Ultimately, the memory that accumulates outcomes of previous experiences and knowledge of situational probabilities strongly affects both attentional control and anticipatory reactions of highly skilled performers (Gold and Shadlen, 2007).

From the viewpoint of neurophysiology, the decision-making process is partly localized in the areas of the medial frontal cortex and the basal ganglia, which supervise areas of the motor response (Yarrow et al., 2009). Moreover, experiments with Transcranial Magnetic Stimulation revealed increased corticospinal facilitation of muscles during imagery of game activity in expert tennis players (Fourkas et al., 2008). This neurophysiological response is sport specific and largely affects choice reactions during the game. It is suggested that skilled athletes can enhance their decision circuits, obtaining a more favorable and quicker response (Gold and Shadlen, 2007).

The above mentioned triad "attention-anticipation-memory" and neural adaptations of brain structures largely determine psychophysiological mechanisms underlying the manifestation and enhancement of complex motor reactions of high-performance athletes.

2.6. Agility

The area of agility manifestation pertains to sport activities demanding rapid changes of whole-body movement direction in predictable and unpredictable situations. This clarification first draws attention to ball games and combat sports, although several sports such as gymnastics, track and field, synchronized swimming, cycling, sailing, alpine and cross-country skiing, etc. also contain similar situations and involve demands of agility manifestation. The classic examples of agility-demanding activities are associated with soccer, where the legendary Pele remains in sport history as one of the most agile players in the World (Figure 7).

Figure 7. Legendary soccer player Pele (Brazil) who demonstrated exceptional football-specific agility

Example of an outstanding athlete. The great Brazilian athlete Pele (Edson Arantes do Nascimento) is usually considered the greatest soccer player of all time. He started his soccer activity in early childhood, however, at age 15 he was already training with a senior team and the local media promoted him as future superstar. Beginning at age 17, Pele was involved with the Brazil National team and took part in the 1958 World Cup where he was the youngest player on any team. His contribution to the victory of the Brazilian team was amazing and Pele was named the greatest revelation of the 1958 World Cup. During subsequent decades, Pele remained in a leading position on the Brazilian team, which won two World Cups. Following the decision of the International soccer federation, Pele was named the greatest player of the 20th century.

The available body of literature and current practice distinguishes between two modes of this CA component:

1. Planned agility: often referred to as Change of Direction Speed (CODS), where an athlete performs a firmly predetermined task with sprints, stops and turns;

2. Reactive agility: where an athlete performs a task that includes introduced stimuli that require an adequate and rapid response (Oliver and Meyers, 2009).

Table 7 introduces a summary of several studies devoted to investigation of athletes' agility.

Table 7. Summary of studies examining agility

Study	Study design	Study outcomes
Gabbett and Benton, 2009	24 elite and 42 sub-elite rugby players underwent reactive agility tests that included reaction to visual stimuli, decision making and speed evaluation	Elite players were significantly superior in decision-making accuracy and speed of movement, which largely affected reactive agility
Chaouachi et al., 2009	14 elite basketball players were tested with regard to planned agility, jump and sprint performances, body composition, VO_2max, 1RM bench press and squat	Planned agility is closely associated with VO_2max and low body fat. Jumping, sprints and strength values don't correlate with agility
Oliver and Meyers, 2009	17 trained male athletes carried out tests of linear sprint, planned and reactive agility	Both planned and reactive agility can be measured with high reliability and sufficient accuracy
Sporiš et al., 2010	80 trained athletes, 2 groups, completed a 10 wk conditioning program. One group underwent 30 agility sessions; control group had no agility workouts	Experimental group manifested significant superiority in jumping performances and 5m sprint. Therefore, agility training largely affected fitness level of power athletes
Serpell et al., 2011	8 trained rugby players underwent a 3 wk reactive agility program to develop perceptual and decision-making ability. 7 other players performed traditional rugby training	Experimental group significantly enhanced reactive agility whereas control group didn't progress. Thus, perceptual and decision-making components are sufficiently trainable
Spiteri et al., 2014	12 elite female basketball players completed tests of planned and reactive agility and measurements of lower body strength	Planned agility highly correlates with lower body strength, whereas reactive agility test had no correlation with this fitness component
Spasic et al., 2015	23 female and 26 male elite handball players underwent tests of planned and reactive agility, measurements of body status and fitness	Ratio between results in tests of planned and reactive agilities characterizes perceptual and reactive capacity and serves as a predictor of real-game agility

The evaluation of reactive agility of rugby players differed by level competence and revealed that elite players have significant superiority compared to their sub-elite counterparts in relation to accuracy, decision making and running speed (Gabbett and Benton, 2009). Study outcomes allowed the researchers to classify the players according to their advantages and disadvantages in several components of reactive agility. A study of elite basketball players revealed a high correlation between planned agility, maximal oxygen uptake, and low percentage of body fat (Chaouachi et al., 2009]. Planned and reactive agility as well as sprint performance were evaluated in trained male volunteers. This study confirmed the sufficient accuracy and reliability of the employed tests; sprint performance was highly correlated with planned but not with reactive agility (Oliver and Meyers, 2009).

Two studies evaluated the effects of special training interventions on the agility performances of qualified athletes. It was established that the inclusion of agility drills into a conditioning program of power athletes resulted in significant improvement in sprint and jumping performance compared to the control group (Sporiš et al., 2010). The effect of a reactive agility program was assessed in an experiment with 2 groups of trained rugby players (Serpell et al., 2011). The study outcomes revealed a significant impact of the experimental program on reactive agility whereas the control group did not obtain any remarkable enhancement.

A parallel investigation of planned and reactive agility revealed that they characterize two separate, specific abilities. A study with elite female basketball players revealed a high dependence of planned agility on lower body strength, while reactive agility had no correlation with these strength variables (Spiteri et al., 2014). Similarly, outcomes of a study with elite female and male handball players revealed that planned and reactive abilities have relatively low correlation. Nevertheless, the relationship between estimates of planned and reactive agility is highly predictive for the characterization of real-game agility (Spasic et al., 2015).

Although several studies reported a moderate to small correlation between power/strength variables and agility (Young et al., 2015) other studies have provided evidence that purposeful agility training produces a significant increase in jumping abilities and lower body power performance (Sporiš et al., 2010). It is likely that although lower body strength/power variables largely contribute to a general fitness background, agility's enhancement is mostly predetermined by properly organized, specialized training with accentuation of sport-specific demands.

Evidentially, the factors affecting the manifestation and enhancement of agility refer to the above considered physical fitness, cognitive and perceptual prerequisites, and training interventions.

It is widely accepted that perceptual-cognitive capacity largely determines agility and its impact may occur in a general or specific mode (Abernethy et al, 1999). General perceptual-cognitive capacity can be realized in a relatively broad domain of expertise without sport-specific context, whereas specific perceptual-cognitive ability relates to proper athletic activity such as real-game or real-race situations. Cognitive skills such as anticipation and decision-making serve as distinct contributors to agility and should be the focus of researchers and practitioners (Paul et al., 2016).

During the recent decades, training interventions have appeared to be valuable resources for the enhancement of agility and include various forms of mental preparation and specially designed training drills. Various applications of mental training have utilized demonstrations with a video clip with an appropriate, pre-programmed scenario; the athletes were required to react quickly and accurately, during a restricted time span, in an agility-demanding, mental task (Blumenstein and Orbach, 2012). In all cases, these mental interventions led to substantial improvement in real-game agility.

Another type of training intervention is associated with modeling of agility-demanding situations in specially designed drills. Experiences of advanced practice and studies in team sports have shown the high effectiveness of small-sided games, which provide a conjugated impact on the coordinative, technical and physical abilities of the athletes (Hill-Haas et al., 2011). Their benefits are reasonably attributed to the increased intensity of game activities, accentuated interaction with partners and opponents, higher demands to decision-making actions, and involvement of cognitive and technical skills. The superiority of training programs with small-sided games compared to traditional training design has been proven in an appropriate study (Owen et al., 2014).

From the viewpoint of neurophysiology, special attention should be given to the positive impact of agility training on cognitive functions (Lennemann et al., 2013). Furthermore, studies on animal models have revealed that agility training produces increased neurogenesis and synaptogenesis in the motor cortex (Kleim et al., 2002). Therefore, large areas of brain are involved in the neural regulation of agility-demanding activities.

2.7. Balance ability

The spectrum of balance ability applications encompasses a multitude of implications to various programs of performance enhancement, prevention of injuries and rehabilitation. Two modes of body balance are distinguished and evaluated. Static balance is characterized as the ability to maintain a stable body position with minimal displacement of body limbs and center of gravity; dynamic balance is considered the ability to perform a motor task while maintaining a stable body position during stance or moving on an unstable or narrow surface (Hrysomallis, 2011). Manifestation of body balance includes a multitude of sport-specific situations that are realized both in terrestrial and aquatic conditions. It is commonly accepted that gymnasts and rifle shooters have the highest level of body balance (Hrysomallis, 2011). In addition, superior balance ability serves as a distinct determinant of technical skills in various activities such as ball games, combat sports, figure skating, ice hockey, etc. Nevertheless, artistic gymnastics presents the most representative setting of elements demanding both static and dynamic body balance, where one apparatus called the "balance beam" presupposes the most accentuated manifestation of this coordination ability (Figure 8).

Figure 8. Execution of unique balance element on the "balance beam" by many-fold Olympic Champion Olga Korbut (USSR)

Example of an outstanding athlete. Olga Korbut remains in the history of contemporary sport as one of the most famous and creative representatives of artistic gymnastics. She started regular training at age 8. At age 14, Olga acquired and performed, for first time in the world, a new element – a backward somersault on the balance beam. One year later, she won her 1st gold medal in the USSR senior championships. At age 17, Olga earned 3 gold medals at the 1972 Munich Olympic Games in the balance beam, the floor exercise, and as a USSR team member. Olga earned one more Olympic gold medal in the 1976 Montreal Olympics. The original elements that she developed and implemented on the balance beam and uneven bars are referred to as the Korbut Flip. A wax figure of Olga Korbut on the balance beam is presented at Madame Tussauds museum in London.

The evaluation of body balance requires the employment of appropriate motor trials separately for static and dynamic modalities. The most widely used laboratory test prescribes the registration of displacements of the center of pressure on a force platform while maintaining a motionless, unilateral or bilateral position with open or closed eyes (Guskiewicz and Perrin, 1996). The research practice utilizes precise instruments such as the Biodex Balance System, which contains a movable platform with programmed levels of oscillations and measurements of deviations from the horizontal level (Arnold and Schmtz, 1998).

The investigation of balance ability traditionally raises vivid interest of both researchers and practitioners (Table 8).

Table 8. Summary of studies examining balance ability

Study	Study design	Study outcomes
Paillard et al., 2002	Static balance of 11 elite and 9 sub-elite judo athletes was examined on a force platform in a standing position for 50s with eyes open and closed	Elite and sub-elite athletes had superior balance with open but not with closed eyes. Visual control highly contributes to balance ability of judo athletes
Kovacs et al., 2004	22 trained figure skaters completed 4 weeks of off-ice training to improve neuromuscular control and balance during landing. Control group (n=22) performed basic fitness program	Experimental group obtained significant superiority in static balance and in a landing jump test with closed eyes. Off-ice neuromuscular training largely enhanced postural control of skaters
Paillard et al., 2006	15 elite and 15 sub-elite soccer players were examined in a unilateral position for static (stable ground) and dynamic (seesaw device) balance with open and closed eyes	Elite players produced better static and dynamic balance than sub-elite athletes. In all cases, lack of vision aggravated balance although elite players were more dependent on visual control
Taube et al., 2007	17 elite athletes were assigned to balance (BT) or strength (ST) training programs for 6 wks. Strength tests, jump performances and H-reflex recruitment were evaluated	Both groups enhanced jump abilities, but maximal strength increased in ST group only. In BT group spinal excitability decreased, indicating improvement of movement control
Granacher &, Gollhofer, 2011	28 adolescent athletes underwent assessment of static and dynamic balance on force platform, jumping abilities, maximal isometric leg force and rate of force development	No significant correlations were found between static and dynamic balance, and strength/power variables. Thus, general fitness doesn't affect balance but is important for injury prevention
Matthews et al., 2016	11 trained female martial arts athletes completed a 4 week program for dynamic balance. Control group (n=12) performed traditional training	Experimental group significantly enhanced dynamic balance. Control group didn't change balance performance

A comparison of elite judo athletes with sub-elite counterparts revealed their significant superiority in static balance with open but not with closed eyes (Paillard et al., 2002). Apparently, visual control of elite judokas largely enhances their balance ability during the fight. Similar outcomes were obtained in a study with elite and sub-elite soccer players where more proficient athletes showed more efficient involvement of visual information in motor tasks demanding both static and dynamic balance (Paillard et al., 2006).

The effect of purposeful, sport-specific balance training was examined in a well controlled study with two groups of trained figure skaters (Kovacs et al., 2004). One group completed four weeks of an off-ice program directed toward the enhancement of postural control in balance exercises and specifically during landing simulation, whereas the control group executed traditionally designed training. The experimental program resulted in significantly superior enhancement of body balance both in off-ice tests and in skating performance.

Another example of successful sensorimotor training was realized in a study with young elite ski jumpers and cross-country skiers (Taube et al., 2007). The protocol utilized a six week program directed toward balance training in one group and a program directed toward strength abilities in another group. Both groups enhanced their jump performances, whereas strength abilities were improved only in the second but not in the balance group. However, the evaluation of H-reflex recruitment allowed the researchers to find decreased spinal excitability in the balance group and, therefore, the sensorimotor training evoked more efficient movement control. These findings are consistent with data from a study with female martial-artists who significantly enhanced their dynamic balance following four weeks of purposeful balance training (Matthews et al., 2016).

The investigation of static and dynamic balance of trained adolescent athletes did not reveal a correlation of these abilities with jumping performance or strength/power variables (Granacher and Gollhofer, 2011). These data are consistent with recent findings that revealed various fitness estimates restrictedly affect the balance abilities of athletes (Muehlbauer et al., 2013).

Considering the above reviewed papers, three important circumstances should be emphasized. First, both static and dynamic balance abilities are sufficiently trainable; correspondingly, the involvement of appropriate task-oriented, selective exercises is highly recommended. Secondly, highly professional, long-term athletic preparation in body-balance-demanding sports produces remarkable improvement of these abilities, obtaining a superior level in elite athletes. Third, balance abilities and general fitness characteristics of athletes have a relatively low correlation and are relatively independent. Correspondingly, balance abilities require properly organized training, which also has a high value for injury prevention (Zech et al., 2010).

Although the neural mechanisms underlining the development and refinement of balance abilities remain under debate, their basic presumptions can be proposed. Proprioceptive control is widely considered an indispensable part of the sensory system that provides an athlete with information on joint motions and body position during the execution of a balance task (Zemková, 2009; Zech et al., 2010). The availability of sensory cues makes it possible produce rational motor responses and to refine a balance skill.

Furthermore, it is proposed that balance training suppresses the excitability of the muscle stretch reflex and enhances agonist-antagonist interactions, providing increased joint stiffness. This inhibition of spinal reflexes allows an athlete to stabilize a joint's position against perturbations. Moreover, purposeful balance training reduces cortical excitability and movement control descends from cortical to subcortical and cerebellar structures (Taube et al., 2008). This shift makes balance regulation more reliable and autonomic.

Summarizing this section, we can claim that basic CA cover a large spectrum of professionally important qualities of both youth and adult athletes. Although their manifestation is closely associated with heredity-related factors, a multitude of findings demonstrate the high extent of trainability in various components of coordination competence. Further sections of this book will present additional information that should allow for better understanding and administration of training directed toward enhancement of the coordination potential of athletes.

Chapter 3 - Hereditary and environmental factors of Coordination Abilities

This chapter is focused on heredity-related and environmental prerequisites of CA; by "environmental" we mean that their manifestation and progression is strictly determined following purposeful, systematic training. Hereditary properties are extremely important for recognition of gifted youngsters whereas environmental factors determine the effectiveness of general and sport-specific preparation both of youth and adult athletes. Their consideration has high practical importance.

3.1. Genetic determination of Coordination Abilities

Quantitative estimation of inheritance, which is very sophisticated, makes it possible to answer how genetic factors contribute to the development of CA. Correspondingly, we can expect higher or lower levels of trainability for various CA components. The most widely used method to assess the inheritance of several traits is the twins' investigation. In general, the idea behind the twins' method is based on the comparison of identical (monozygotic) twins to fraternal (dizygotic) twins. Because monozygotic twins have identical heredity, all differences in their capabilities are attributed exclusively to the influence of the environment. Dizygotic twins share one-half of their genes, so their heredity is different but environmental conditions are usually identical. In this case, any differences in a trait observed between them must be attributed to heredity. The quantitative estimate of the effect of heredity is *heritability*, which characterizes the degree of genetic determination of several traits.

Despite the obvious difficulties, the twins' studies form an extensive and very informative branch of sports science that presents valuable knowledge related to heritability of various fitness qualities. Special attention should be given to the hereditary aspects of CA, of which the contribution to the acquisition and perfection of technical motor skills cannot be underestimated. An extensive review of numerous studies was fulfilled by Lyakh with coworkers (2007). Despite the fact that several research groups presented contradictory findings, the general tendencies of coordinative inheritance can be specified (Table 9).

Table 9

Hereditary characteristics of several coordination abilities

(based on Lyakh et al, 2007)

Characteristics	General genetic control	Levels of inheritance
Spatial orientation	strong	60-70%
Kinaesthetic differentiation	medium	~ 40%
Eye-hand coordination	moderate	~ 30%
Movement frequency (speed)	moderate	~ 30%
Static body balance	medium	~ 40%
Dynamic body balance	moderate	~ 30%

The general conclusion that can be drawn from Table 9 is that coordination abilities, with the exception of spatial orientation, have moderate to low genetic control and, therefore, are sufficiently trainable. Nevertheless, the data from rare studies have shown a more sophisticated perspective. Namely, Ljach (2002) studied the speed of complex motor reaction in children 7-9 years of age and found that this functional ability is strongly determined by heredity. This fact seems very important with regard to the world-wide practice of coordination training of children aged 5-9 years in such sports as gymnastics, figure skating, etc. Moreover, they revealed significant correlations between CA of parents and children (about 0.50). Interestingly, similar coefficients of correlation were also found relating to intellect. Apparently, indicators of CA can be used as early predictors of athletic giftedness and talent.

The available data provide evidence that the rate of coordinative improvement is much less dependent on hereditary factors than on CA themselves and, therefore, are sufficiently trainable (Lyalh, 2006). This fact provides distinct support for the implementation of a rational training methodology and emphasizes its importance for the preparation of youth and adult athletes. Evidently, high learnability can be reasonably considered a valuable indicator of athletic giftedness. However, the level of motor learnability can be assessed after some period of preliminary training. At the initial stage of athlete selection, special attention should be given to spatial orientation, kinaesthetic differentiation with regards to angular displacements and force application, and complex motor reaction. After 1-2 years of purposeful preparation, motor learnability can be successfully evaluated, having a highly predictive value.

It is worth noting that the determination of hereditary prerequisites is particularly important for highly coordinative, esthetic sports such as gymnastics, figure skating, synchronized swimming, etc. Children begin preparation in these sports at ages 4-5 and usually have no experience in other sports. In this case, hereditary predisposition can be more successfully evaluated. In ball games, combat sports, rowing, kayaking, etc. children start preparation at ages 12-14, having substantial experience in various sport activities. Correspondingly, outcomes of their motor trials strongly depend on previous experiences and available motor skills. In this case, coordinative diagnostics can largely assist in revealing their inborn prerequisites for a given sport.

3.2. Additional factors affecting Coordination Abilities of athletes

As it was proposed in the previous section, basic CA are substantially associated with heredity-transmitted factors. Indeed, such heredity-related properties as sensorimotor reactions, perception, cognitive abilities and particularities of the central nervous system can largely determine general learnability and acquisition of new motor skills. Although a major portion of basic CA have a medium to moderate level of inheritance, the role of genetic determination of coordination competence cannot be underestimated. From a scientific and practical viewpoint, such additional factors as somatic variables, physical fitness and experience in various motor activities may raise particular interest.

The findings of several studies show low to moderate correlations between basic CA and somatic variables of adult athletes (Sheppard and Young, 2006; Hrysomallis, 2011). However, investigations of youth athletes revealed significant relationships between body size and coordinative competence at ages 7-10, 11-14 and 15-17 (Lyakh, 2006). Perhaps this can be explained by fact that more mature individuals have both larger body size and a more favorable background of physical activity. Further athletic preparation may eliminate these differences in training experiences and coordination capacity of junior athletes. Purposeful preparation in such sports as basketball, volleyball, throwing disciplines, etc. provides distinct advantages to more robust and larger individuals, who obtain a higher level of sport-specific skills and basic CA. On the other hand, such sports as gymnastics and diving provide benefits for small-sized athletes, who may attain an exceptional level of coordination competence. The somatic variables strongly affect the development of sport-specific CA and skills, whereas their influence on basic CA is less deterministic and depends on many individual factors.

Research findings have shown significant relationships between basic CA and fitness variables in children and adolescents. It was revealed that their results in maximal speed and speed-strength trials largely affected the manifestation of various basic CA, whereas estimates of endurance and flexibility have shown low or non-significant influence (Lyakh, 2006). Evidently, the physiological background of CA and physical fitness variables is very different. This particularity demands the administration of separate training programs for stimulation of CA and sport-specific motor fitness. Of course, from a distinct perspective, the conjugate training approach combines the development of coordinative and fitness components (Verkhoshansky, 2006).

Another factor affecting the manifestation of basic CA is associated with previous motor experience and acquisition of various motor skills during early childhood. Acquisition of such diversified skills may be achieved as a result of appropriate family education, involvement in various informal physical activities (not in organized groups), and earlier involvement in athletic preparation in various sports. Retrospective studies of exceptionally talented athletes who earned the highest Olympic awards revealed that they usually started their athletic activities in early childhood in various sports prior to entering their favorite sport at age 14-18 (Durand-Bush, 2000; Riewald and Snyder, 2014; Issurin, 2017). It can be suggested that this earlier, diversified activity allowed for the development of coordination prerequisites in these outstanding athletes and assisted in their choice of a favorite specialization.

The benefits of earlier coordinative development were revealed in systematic studies conducted in East Germany. Experiments with schoolchildren aged 7-11 years have shown their high trainability in the acquisition of various skills from gymnastics, track and field and ball games (Hirtz, 1985). Correspondingly, the level of basic CA of these purposefully trained children also significantly increased. It is worth noting that acquisition of various specific motor skills occurs successfully within particular groups of athletic activities. Namely, the children experienced in certain ball games acquire technical skills from other ball games at a relatively faster rate. Similarly, children with technical prerequisites in a certain type of cyclic locomotion can successfully utilize skill transfer in other cyclic sport activities. This corresponds to the widely known fact that speed skaters relatively easily acquire skills in cycling. Such positive skill transfer is efficiently used in the learning of throwing disciplines and acquisition of highly coordinated technical elements in gymnastics and acrobatics. In all of these cases, the enhancement of basic CA such as kinaesthetic differentiation, body balance, etc. occurs as an associated outcome of increased coordination capacity.

One more important factor of coordination competence is *motor learnability,* which can be characterized as an important prerequisite for mastering new technical elements in different athletic activities. As it was previously noted, this coordinative ability is largely predetermined by heredity-related factors. Researchers have reasonably assumed that motor learnability largely depends on memory, attention, anticipation, creativity and previous motor experience (Belej and Junger, 2006). Apparently, earlier stimulation of basic CA can substantially reinforce the development of motor learnability in potentially talented individuals and can compensate for deficiencies in less gifted children (Hirtz, 1985; Mekota, 2006).

3.3. Natural Trends in the Development of Basic CA

Multiyear athletic preparation can be considered one of the most influencing environmental factors. From this position, a natural trend in the development of basic CA raises our vivid interest associated with the possible obtainment of techno-tactical mastery in given sport. Although specificity of each sport discipline dictates proper demands to the coordinative profile of athletes, general tendencies of CA development should be outlined and taken into account in training planning and design. Available data allow us to characterize a natural trend in the development of various CA until they obtain the level of maximal realization, i.e. "definitive level" (Table 10).

Table 10. Age when youth athletes obtain 25, 50, 75 and 100% of maximal level of realization of different CA (based on Lyakh, 2006)

Coordination abilities	Gender	25%	50%	75%	100%
Kinaesthetic differentiation	M	7.9	9.3	12.3	17.0
	F	8.4	9.1	12.1	17.0
Rhythmic ability	M	8.3	10.4	12.4	15.3
	F	8.2	9.5	10.3	15.1
Spatial orientation	M	8.2	11.1	13.3	15.5
	F	7.7	10.5	13.1	15.4
Body balance	M	10.8	12.2	12.7	14.5
	F	9.8	11.2	12.1	14.5
Complex motor reaction	M	9.3	9.8	11.5	17.0
	F	8.7	10.0	11.9	14.5
Agility	M	8.1	9.1	10.5	17.0
	F	8.2	9.6	11.4	17.0

This data show that at age 8, children obtain about 25% of the definitive level of basic CA. Body balance can be considered an exception, where this level is achieved later both in boys and girls. Obtaining the level of 50% occurs between 9 and 11 years; the level of 75% is achieved between 10.5 and 13 years. Interestingly, the level of 100% can be obtained at age 15 in body balance, rhythmic ability, and spatial orientation in girls and boys. This level can be achieved at age 17 in such CA as kinaesthetic differentiation and agility in boys and girls; the definitive level of complex motor reaction is obtained in girls at 14.5 and at age 17 in boys. It should be noted that purposeful, specialized training can largely accelerate the development of several CA and allow for achievement of the definitive level much earlier than in the average population. Classic examples of such exceptions can be found in gymnastics and figure skating, where excellent manifestations of body balance, rhythmic ability and agility already occur at ages 13-14.

It is well known that some periods are more favorable for the development of several motor abilities compared to others. These time intervals, termed "sensitive periods," are of special interest for both scientists and practitioners. For CA, sensitive periods include ages 7-10 years (Lyakh, 2006). It is very desirable that during this period, children receive appropriate stimulation of CA using diversified, multilateral motor tasks and various athletic activities. In sports where athletic preparation starts during pre-puberty, such as gymnastics, figure skating and synchronized swimming, training programs provide accentuated development of CA. Thus, in these sports, sensitive periods of CA are efficiently exploited. In other sports such as ball games, combat sports, rowing, etc. athletic preparation usually starts at ages 13-14 and the benefits of higher sensitivity to CA workloads cannot be utilized. Experiences of world-class athletes from these sports show that they usually practiced various sport activities before beginning their favorite sports (Durand-Bush, 2000; Riewald and Snyder, 2014; Issurin, 2017). Apparently this premature athletic practice during the sensitive period produced valuable coordinative prerequisites for subsequent, specialized preparation of these outstanding athletes.

3.4. Gender differentiation in development of basic CA

Gender differences related to CA have certain particularities associated with morphological status and previous athletic experiences of athletes. Girls aged 7-13 demonstrate similar abilities as boys in regards to manifestation of kinaesthetic differentiation, rhythmic ability and static body balance. However, in trials that demand preliminary sport-specific experiences, boys usually have certain advantages. For instance, examination of soccer-related CA in novices revealed that females displayed a relatively lower level than boys in initial performance. However, following purposeful, soccer-specific training, female players diminished their initial disadvantage in rhythmic ability with dribbling and speed of reaction to a rolling ball. Furthermore, females outperformed male players in examinations of kinaesthetic differentiation in shooting with the dominant leg, and static and dynamic body balance. Male players demonstrated superiority in such CA components as agility and spatial orientation (Lyakh, 2006). Apparently, purposeful training reduces gender differences in CA associated with female deficiencies in speed-strength abilities and technical skills.

The graph in Figure 9 displays the longitudinal trend of agility in boys and girls at ages 7-17. The superiority of boys remains significant during the whole period of examination. Apparently the shuttle run (3×10m agility test) that was used depends on general speed-strength prerequisites, where boys have a substantial advantage compared to girls, and this benefit largely determines their superiority. The natural trend of agility in girls displays permanent improvement until age 16. The decrease in agility in girls between 16 and 17 years of age may be associated with increased body weight and reduced physical activity that frequently occurs in non-athletic females. Evidently, regular sport activity produces pronounced improvement rates and affects the increasing superiority of youth athletes compared to non-athletic boys.

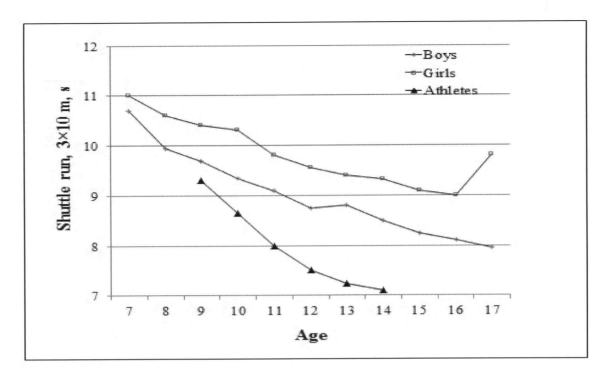

Figure 9. Natural trend of agility in boys and girls from age 7 to 17 as compared to data of youth athletes (based on Lyakh, 2006)

It is worth noting that the self-regulated physical activity of children prior to entering into regular training in organized groups differs between boys and girls. Usually boys have more initiative and are more involved in many outdoor activities; this circumstance may determine their superiority in various CA. From this position, earlier involvement of girls in various sport activities is strongly recommended.

The findings of studies demonstrate that female athletes involved in highly coordinative, esthetic sports obtain a superior level and even outperform male athletes in body balance, kinaesthetic differentiation and rhythmic ability (Hirtz and Starosta , 2002; Lyakh, 2006).

3.5. Longitudinal trends in development of coordinative competence

It is well known that purposeful athletic training produces a distinct impact on the development of basic CA. Available data allow us to characterize the long-term dynamics and improvement rates of different CA during highly dedicated athletic preparation. From this perspective, data of youth ice-hockey players raises particular interest due to the pronounced demands to coordination competence that exist in this team sport.

A special study was conducted in the Slovak Republic where 283 junior athletes (aged 11-15 years) from specialized sport classes were examined (Broďáni and Šimonek, 2012). Basic CA were evaluated using the most popular trials, namely: dynamic balance – performance of three turns on an overturned gymnastics bench (sec); complex motor reaction - stopping a rolling ball (cm); spatial orientation - shuttle run to arbitrary numbered balls (sec); kinesthetic-differentiation of legs - precision standing broad jump (error in cm). The average trends of this data are presented in Figure 10:

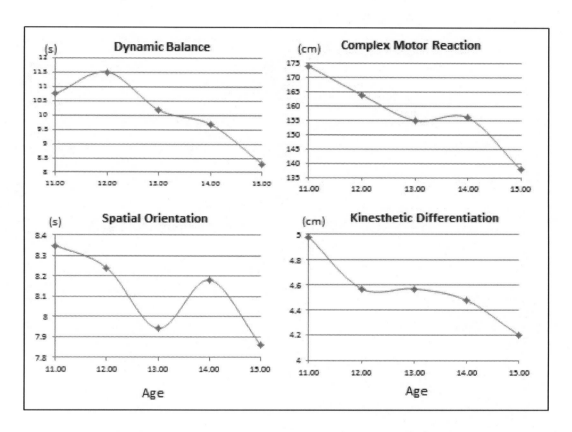

Figure 10. Longitudinal trends of several basic CA of youth ice-hockey players from age 11 to 15 (based on Broďáni and Šimonek, 2012)

The above presented data display complex and non-uniform trends of various CA. For instance, dynamic balance did not improved at age 12 but was substantially enhanced from ages 12 to 15. Similarly, we can mark the stagnation in development of complex motor reaction between 13 and 14 years. Surprisingly, spatial orientation decreased at age 14 with pronounced improvement at age 15. Interestingly, kinaesthetic differentiation reached its highest improvement rate between 11 and 12 years and again between 14 and 15 years. It can be suggested that these noticeable deviations in the development of basic CA are associated with particularities of sport-specific adaptations during long-term preparation in ice-hockey. Accumulation of accentuated training workloads may produce phases of temporal decrease in several CA and delayed effects of pronounced enhancement. Regular monitoring of coordination competence should be an important and compulsory component of the preparation system in both youth and adult athletes.

3.6. Improvement of coordination competence of high-performance athletes

Successful attempts to implement purposeful coordination programs into the preparation of qualified athletes were realized in different sports aiming to improve the quality of training and competition performance. In all cases, coordination training was incorporated into the preparation program and was realized in the linkage with fitness and technical routines; the effectiveness of competition performances was evaluated using sport-specific criteria that are relevant in world practice (Table 11).

Table 11. Summary of studies devoted to examination of coordination programs

Sample	Study design	Gains of various factors (%)				Sources
		CA	Technical mastery	Fitness abilities	Competition performance	
Basketball, 13 girls aged 13-14 yrs	Program of CA stimulation, 2 years	35.2	36.3	12.0	86.3	Mikolajec, Ljakh, 1998
Basketball, 16 girls aged 17 yrs	Program of CA stimulation, 2 years	18.2	19.3	17.5	18.9	Mikolajec, Ljakh, 1998
Tae kwon do, 18-29 yrs, 15 men, 13 women	Program of CA stimulation, two years	26.7	24.0	9.7	20.9 –men; 27.5-women	Sadowski, 2000
Greco-Roman wrestlers, 18-19 yrs, n-16	Program of CA stimulation, half year, 84 sessions	4.7	6.9	3.3	53.1	Gierzuk, 2004
Freestyle wrestlers, 18-19 yrs, n-13	Program of CA stimulation, half year, 84 sessions	5.7	10.8	5.7	42.4	Gierzuk, 2004

The findings of the above studies revealed a considerable increase in technical mastery following the inclusion of coordination programs. Employment of appropriate sport-specific trials allowed researchers to also demonstrate the progression of relevant fitness characteristics. Moreover, in all cases, the athletes substantially enhanced their competitive performance. It is worth noting that coordination sessions were included 2-3 times a week for 15-20min immediately after warming up or in the conclusive part of the workout. Notably, this relatively small training volume sufficiently influenced technical abilities and competitive performance. Apparently the included exercises that were directed toward enhancement of basic CA provided remarkable positive training transfer on technical abilities of subjects. Relatively long periods of training interventions provided sufficient accumulation of a positive stimulatory effect that resulted in a significant improvement in competition performance.

Interestingly, basketball players and tae kwon do athletes have shown much more pronounced gains in CA as compared with their improvement in fitness abilities (Mikolajec and Ljakh, 1998; Sadowski, 2000). These proportions were not supported by study outcomes with wrestlers, who had a relatively higher initial level of coordination competence and, therefore, were less sensitive to the coordinative interventions (Gierzuk, 2004). Nevertheless these highly qualified athletes obtained very impressive enhancement in their sport-specific, competitive activity, which was much more successful than during previous preparation. Evidentially, the inclusion of coordination programs produced a valuable stimulatory impact on both fitness and technical components of their professional preparedness.

Chapter 4 - Methodological aspects of purposeful development of Coordination Abilities

This chapter presents relevant information related to the principles, training approaches and planning basics for the purposeful preparation of athletes aiming to provide a pronounced effect from high quality, coordination training. The long-term experiences of prominent coaches and findings of previous studies allowed us to propose a number of principles that should be realized during the compilation of preparation programs directed toward improvement of coordination competence and sport-specific preparedness in youth and adult high-performance athletes. They are:

- Coordination training should be an indispensable part of the whole preparation system,
- Stimulation of basic CA should be integrated into technical preparation,
- Application of the coordination program should accentuate individual strengths and properties of athletes,
- Coordination program should be closely connected with conditioning training,
- Monitoring of basic CA should be implemented into the entire preparation system.

These principles were successfully realized in a number of studies (Table 11); the materials in this chapter provide additional support for their better comprehension and practical application.

4.1. Training approaches realized in the development of basic CA

The available findings demonstrate three principal approaches, which were realized in the development of basic athletic CA. The first one presupposes complex, concurrent enhancement of many CA in the framework of purposeful sport-specific, techno-tactical preparation (1); the second one proposes accentuated training stimulation of properly selected CA that have particular importance for a certain athletic activity (2), and realization of prospective programs that include coordination training as one of the most meaningful and important components of long-term preparation (3).

4.1.1. Concurrent enhancement of many CA

Practical needs often dictate necessity of concurrent training stimulation of many CA. Such an approach is very typical for the preparation of junior and medium level athletes who should increase their general level of coordination competence. The outcomes of a study that was conducted in soccer can be used as an example of successful realization of this approach (Ljach and Witkowski, 2010). 51 highly qualified youth soccer players were subdivided into two groups where the experimental group (EG) was focused on the complex development of basic CA coupled with the execution of appropriately selected technical drills, whereas the control group realized a traditional program for soccer preparation. The one year training program included a coordination intervention for the EG that lasted 6-8min per session, 5-6 sessions per week, for a total of 480min per year. Realization of the experimental program resulted in attainment of significant superiority of the EG in trials of basic CA, principal technical elements, and soccer performance.

Another example pertains to a study that was conducted with 32 highly qualified Greco-Roman wrestlers aiming to specify a rational distribution of training means directed toward the development of basic and sport-specific CA during annual athletic preparation (Gierczuk and Bujak, 2013). The study design presupposed allocation of 31% of total time expenses during pre-season preparation and 23% of the training time during the in-season period for coordination training. The maximum time expenses were directed toward development of basic and sport-specific agility (40-50%). Coordination routines for the enhancement of rhythmic abilities varied within 20-30%; the least amount of training time was devoted to spatial orientation (10%) and complex motor reaction (10%). Improvement of kinaesthetic differentiation occurred at the low end of this ranking (5%). Apparently this time distribution reasonably reflected the sport-specific demands for attainment of the desired standard of techno-tactical mastery in proficient Greco-Roman wrestlers and led to significant enhancement of their CA, fighting skills and athletic performance.

This training strategy has a broad application for various sports where different CA are highly important for the attainment of a proficient level of techno-tactical mastery.

4.1.2. Selectively accentuated development of certain CA

This training strategy presupposes selectively accentuated development of certain CA that have a particular contribution to the attainment of a higher level of techno-tactical mastery in a given sport. This situation may occur in team sports, where pronounced stimulation of agility can reinforce the performance of techno-tactical skills (Paul et al., 2016). Similarly, pronounced balance training largely contributes to injury prevention (Hrysomallis, 2011).

Tables 7 and 8 provide examples of selective enhancement of agility and body balance, respectively. One more example relates to the development of soccer-specific agility. Such a study was conducted with sub-elite, preadolescent soccer players aiming to evaluate the effectiveness of a 12-week training program directed toward improving soccer-specific agility (Trecroci et al., 2016). The program for the experimental group involved 24 training sessions that included 10min phases of accentuated agility and sprint intervention, whereas the program for the control group completely corresponded to a commonly accepted standard. Study outcomes revealed significant superiority of the experimental group in tests of reactive agility, maximal speed and game performance. Therefore, the goal-oriented agility program provided a distinct, positive effect on their athletic competence.

Another example of reasonable prioritization of CA can be taken from a study with preadolescent tennis players with training experience of 2-5 years (Zetou et al., 2012). The 48 participants in this study were randomly separated into two groups. The experimental group's 5 week program focused on exercises directed toward the development of tennis-specific kinaesthetic differentiation and reaction ability. The control group's program did not provide any prioritization for several CA. After completion of the experimental program, analysis of pre-post gains revealed significant superiority of the experimental group in performance of primary technical elements such as service.

Evidentially, both of the above considered training strategies have proper benefits, limitations and perspectives.

4.2. Planning of coordination training in the framework of multiyear preparation

Although coordination training is an indispensable part of athletic preparation, its contribution to the overall program during different stages of long-term preparation requires clarification. Correspondingly, rational proportions of coordination, conditioning and techno-tactical components of the program deserve concrete characterization (Table 12).

Table 12. Proposed proportions between main training components (in %) during long-term athletic preparation (based on Lyakh, 2009)

Age	Coordination training	Conditioning training	Technical preparation	Tactical preparation
8-10	30	30	30	10
11-12	20	30	35	15
13-14	20	25	35	20
15-16	20	25	30	25
17-18	15	25	30	30

The offered proportions of coordination, conditioning and techno-tactical preparation pertain to ball games and combat sports where coordination is of particular importance. Its contribution to overall training time expenses appears to be greater in the initial stage of long-term preparation and decreases during more specialized stages where the role and importance of sport-specific, techno-tactical preparation reasonably increases (Lyach, 2009). It is worth noting that between the ages of 8 and 10 is characterized as one of the most favorable for the development of CA and is considered a "sensitive period" (Hirtz and Starosta , 2002). The growth spurt associated with puberty occurs between ages 10.5-12.5 in girls and 12.5-14.5 in boys and negatively affects coordination development. The high contribution of coordination training in the early stage of multiyear preparation should produce a general background for further specialization, whereas accentuated stimulation of basic CA during subsequent stages of preparation should compensate for the impairing effect of the growth spurt during post-puberty. Further preparation of matured athletes of 15-18 years old should still contain a coordination program that corresponds to the current demands of sport-specific, techno-tactical mastery and athletic performance.

4.3. Primary directions of CA development in different ages

This subsection summarizes the most generalized positions related to the primary directions of coordination training during different stages of multiyear preparation of athletes in various sports. Although chronological details of long-term preparation largely depend on the specificity of different sports, general positions can be proposed. Of course, in highly coordination esthetic sports such as gymnastics, figure skating, synchronized swimming, etc., the athletes begin purposeful preparation at ages 4-6 and guidelines for coordination training should be appropriately adapted. Nevertheless, in many sport activities such as ball games, combat, endurance, power sports and track and field, the initial purposeful preparation starts at ages 12-14 and later. In many cases, the outstanding athletes from these sports exploit a sensitive period for the development of a coordination background using athletic preparation in other sport activities prior to entering to their favorite sport (Moesch et al.,2011; Riewald and Snyder, 2014; Issurin, 2017). This tendency is supported by evidence from the preparation of 15 Olympic champions in sprint running (Lombardo and Deaner, 2014) and 18 Olympic champions in rowing (Guellich, 2013), who had preliminary preparation experience in 1-3 other sports before they began purposeful preparation in sports where they achieved world-class status. Evidentially, this efficient, specialized preparation presupposes the availability of sufficient coordination prerequisites that are obtained as a result of diversified preliminary training. In many cases, this coordination background may be obtained using athletic activities other than their favorite sports.

Of course the primary directions, content and particularities of coordination training programs are largely dependent on age, qualification and the sport-specific details of the athletes. However, methodological aspects of coordination training require serious clarification. The available literature does not provide comprehensive guidelines that may assist the coaches in the construction of efficient coordination programs. Moreover, selection and compilation of appropriate coordination exercises still remains a prerogative of creative coaches, who solve this problem following their experience, intuition and traditions in certain sports. Although the second part of this book presents a vast array of coordination exercises for different needs, an introduction of the principal positions for the compilation and implementation of goal-directed training means appears both useful and reasonable (Table 13).

Table 13. Development of CA in different ages

Age group	Main directions of CA development	Comments
7-10 years (preliminary and initial athletic preparation)	Achievement of broad coordination basis. Enhancement of kinaesthetic differentiation, rhythmic ability and body balance. Formation of cognitive, sensory-motor and intellectual background of movements, motor memory and imagination	Development of CA using cyclic and acyclic locomotion, throwing exercises, elements from gymnastics and acrobatics, free playing activities, employment of sport games.
11-15 years (specialized athletic preparation)	Further enlargement of coordination basis, acquisition of new motor skills. Further improvement of rhythmic ability, spatial orientation, body balance and voluntary muscular relaxation. Enhancement of special functions such as sense of ball, sense of time, distance and effort. Improvement of motor memory and sport intelligence.	They have a working skills' repertoire in their favorite sport and broad settings of various exercises combined with additional resistance using also various devises such as skis, skates, bicycle, boat, gymnastic apparatus, etc.
16-18 years (further athletic perfection)	Achievement of multilateral coordinative competence predominantly for their selected favorite sport. Further enrichment of the repertoire of diversified motor skills. Enhancement of sport-specific psychophysiological functions associated with mnemonics, motor imagery, creativity and sport intelligence.	Administration of diversified, sport-specific coordination tasks in combination with various fitness and techno-tactical exercises. Employment of unusual motor skills, monitoring of basic CA.

The content of diversified training during initial preparation should be oriented toward the formation of a broad coordination basis and acquisition of general and sport-specific motor skills. Having sufficient coordination competence, the athletes can efficiently build and improve their techno-tactical abilities in their favorite sport. Therefore, a well balanced program should include various motor tasks that support and enlarge the general coordination capacity. Such coaching strategy presupposes utilization of various training means and devices, game activities and original drills from other sports.

The next stage of multiyear preparation is devoted to specialized athletic training. Correspondingly, the preparation program of athletes contains sport-specific settings of specialized exercises and quasi-competitive tasks. However, the inclusion of generalized coordination exercises and tasks is still strongly recommended. Such a program's diversification facilitates recovery after intense and severe workloads, allows for the enrichment of motor experience, and supports general coordination competence. Moreover, systematic monitoring of basic CA can serve as an efficient part of a complex follow-up program.

The third stage of further athletic perfection is directed toward the attainment of pure techno-tactical mastery in the favorite sport. Correspondingly, the program should contain a broad group of appropriate, sport-specific exercises, simulation of competitive activities, and enhancement of psychophysiological prerequisites of athletic mastery. Additional tasks with accentuated coordination demands should be oriented to improve the abilities of attention, motor memory and motor imagery. As a result, the athletes should increase the level of their creativity and sport intelligence.

4.4. Selection and compilation of coordination exercises

Although many creative coaches successfully develop general and sport-specific coordination abilities of their athletes, the selection and compilation of appropriate exercises remains a challenge for both practice and training methodology. Therefore, offering some general rules makes sense both for better understanding and for practical needs (Table 14).

Table 14. Compilation of coordination exercises with strictly preplanned content

No	Preplanned movements variation	Example
1	Changing of movement direction	Dribbling changing direction following given marks, "slalom" exercises
2	Variation of force application	Throwing of different weights with maximal, submaximal and medium effort
3	Changing of speed, movement rate and rhythm of performance	Execution of exercise with acceleration, deceleration or in preplanned rhythm
4	Changing of initial body position	Running starts from sitting, lying or backward position
5	Changing of body position during performance	Catching and throwing the ball in a sitting or lying position
6	Changing of spatial borders of performance	Playing soccer or basketball on smaller field
7	Variation of technical details of performance	Ball shooting using different techniques from different distances
8	Insertion of an additional task that complicates performance	Catching the ball with jump, jump with rotation, etc.
9	Linkage of familiar technical elements in unusual combination	Linkage of a number of acrobatic stunts with agility performance
10	Mirror performance of familiar motor task	Throwing tasks performed by non-dominant arm or leg
11	Insertion of sudden command demanding changing of motor behavior	Rapid transition from defensive to offensive action following command of a coach
12	Execution of technical element in fatigued state	Ball shooting performance after completed soccer match
13	Execution of technical element without visual control	Throwing, jumping and/or shooting performances based on automatized skill and motor memory
14	Execution of technical element with preplanned counteraction of opponent	Such exercises are very typical in combat sports and ball games

Various exercises with changing of movement direction are very typical for the development of agility; they are highly recommended for coordination training in ball games. Such drills can be modified using sudden stops, side steps, jumps and backward running. Exercises for athletes from combat sports can include several sport-specific technical elements. These exercises can be part of a fitness program while controlling performance time, heart rate and blood lactate.

Variations of force application are very useful and efficient for enhancement of kinaesthetic differentiation. Such exercises can include jumps and weight throws of a predetermined distance with and without visual control. Using objective indicators of accuracy allows for efficient improvement of proprioceptive motor control, which is very important for the execution of sport-specific technical elements.

Changing of speed, movement rate and rhythm of performance during preplanned motor tasks allows for the improvement of general rhythmic ability. These exercises can also include additional sport-specific tasks such as jumps, dribbling, ball shooting, etc. When an exercise is performed with increased intensity using the interval method, an appropriate metabolic effect should be expected.

Changing of the initial body position allows for diversification of coordination demands. Administration of a running start from sitting, lying and backward positions provides a stimulation effect for the improvement of complex motor reaction and general agility. Similarly, changing of body position during performance inserts additional coordination demands. Namely, variations of body position during jumping, ball shooting and throwing allow a coach to extend the coordination program, enrich the motor experience, and enhance spatial orientation.

Changing of spatial borders of athletic activity is widely used, particularly in ball games. Reduction of game field size causes more frequent execution of technical elements, closer interaction with partners, and more accentuated counteraction of opponents. This mode of training provides enhancement of sport-specific technical skills, agility and spatial orientation. Using an enlarged game field is less popular and makes sense for accentuated stimulation of sport-specific endurance.

Variation of technical details of performance can be used to accentuate some technical elements, enrich the motor experience and activate proprioceptive motor control of the movement. This variation can be achieved using additional resistance, weighting the body and body segments, execution of movement with preplanned restrictions, using additional devices like fins in swimming, uphill and downhill running, etc. Utilization of different techniques of ball shooting is part of sport-specific preparation in ball games. Similarly, the insertion of an additional task into a customary exercise and linkage of familiar technical elements in an unusual combination allows for modification of performance, an increase in its complexity, and emphasis on coordination demands.

Mirroring performance of a familiar motor task presupposes its execution using a non-dominant arm or leg. This approach is widely used in ball games and combat sports. Evidentially, enriching the technical settings in these sports allows athletes to attain a higher level of technical mastery or, at least, obtain higher stability in performance elements when using their dominant arm or leg. It can be suggested that positive skill transfer from the non-dominant to dominant link reinforces the coordination structure of the dominant links' skill.

Exercises with insertion of a sudden command demanding a change in motor behavior can positively affect basic CA such as complex motor reaction, agility and spatial orientation. Additional tasks for dynamic body balance can be reasonably included in the exercise program.

Execution of technical elements in a fatigued state may produce a conjugate effect on general fitness and fatigue tolerance of the appropriate motor skill. Apparently, the manifestation of efficient motor skills in a real competitive situation can be associated with the ability to tolerate fatigue. Therefore, appropriate exercises should be incorporated into the coordination training program.

Execution of technical elements without visual control is used for purposeful stimulation of proprioceptive motor control and motor memory. Although several highly coordinative motor skills are automatized, reinforced proprioceptive control may largely contribute to increased performance quality.

Execution of technical elements with preplanned counteraction of an opponent also produces a conjugate effect on both the sport-specific skill and the fitness component that is responsible for the execution of this exercise. Preparation in combat sports actively exploits this approach in conditioning and techno-tactical programs.

In addition to the above considered approaches to the compilation of exercises with strictly preplanned content of activity, a special group is formed by exercises with relatively free scenarios where the behavior of athletes is not strictly predetermined. These exercises provide more possibilities for initiative and individual creativity of athletes. Examples of such coordination tasks are presented below:

a)   Execution of various techno-tactical tasks in unusual external conditions such as ball dribbling in the forest, jumps in sand, running in shallow water, etc.

b)   Execution of very familiar exercises using unusual equipment such as balls of different size and weight, throwing of stones and non-standard weights, using an unfamiliar gymnastics apparatus, etc.

c)   Ball games with unfamiliar partners, using an unusual playing position, fighting against different athletes or changing the opponents in combat sports.

d)   Execution of various technical elements with short intervals while varying the sequencing, number of repetitions, and intensity.

In addition, widely used sport practice includes the utilization of motor imagery when athletes mentally reproduce the performance of a certain motor task while focusing on the most relevant details and characteristics. This mental performance can be efficiently combined with real execution and control of the coach (Blumenstein and Orbach, 2012).

Concluding this section, special attention should be given to the utilization of the method of *conjugate training* that presupposes concurrent enhancement of technical skill and appropriate physical abilities in the same exercise. The typical examples of such an approach relate to high quality technical exercises performed with greater force application. In these cases, the concurrent impact on technical skill and sport-specific strength can be provided. Similarly, the conjugate training approach can combine several technical skills and various fitness components such as strength, explosive strength, strength endurance, speed, and flexibility.

4.5. Implementation of different forms of training sessions in the preparation program

There are three basic forms of implementation of CA training in the preparation programs of youth and adult athletes. They are the following:

1) Inclusion of a CA session into a workout of a certain group using appropriate equipment, control and external motivation. This session can be planned for the initial part of the workout, aiming to activate and diversify the program and exploit a higher sensitivity for the acquisition of new motor skills. Administration of a CA session during the basic portion of the training session makes sense if the coach intends to emphasize its role and priority within this workout and provide pronounced stimulation for coordination competence. Inclusion of the CA session at the end of the workout allows the athletes to accomplish the coordination program and purposefully improve fatigue tolerance during the coordination drills. An additional goal could be associated with the achievement of better recovery after preceding workloads. In this case, the session's program should include exercises for voluntary muscle relaxation, flexibility and breathing.

2) Administration of an individual CA session aiming to enhance properly selected abilities and skills that have particular importance for a certain athlete. Such individual sessions, performed with supervision of the coach, usually include goal-directed, techno-tactical tasks with special cues and evaluation of performance quality. Implementation of such an approach is typical for more qualified athletes and serves as a valuable tool for refining their techno-tactical mastery.

3) Giving of an additional task for independent, home preparation according to individual needs and available conditions for exercise execution. In this case, the trainee should receive a detailed prescription of the home task and recommendations for self-control. Individual tasks may also reasonably include motor imagery of several coordination exercises. Such individual training is particularly suitable for vacation and periods when the athlete moves to another place without the coach.

Summary

Available data, evidence, knowledge and experience allow us to describe and properly consider general positions related to Coordination Abilities of athletes. The importance of these positions is widely acknowledged, although their characterization in textbooks and coaching guidelines is far from complete. In fact, coordination training still remains an area of coaching that is based on common sense, intuition, proper experience and traditions of the specific sport. A similar situation occurred with strength and endurance training a few decades ago. The sharing of new knowledge and advanced technologies radically changed this situation. Coordination training deserves a similar progression, both in educational and practical branches.

Clear understanding and adoption of the theory of multilevel construction of human movements opens up a new perspective in the teaching and refining of motor skills. The first chapter of this book introduces this practically-oriented theory proposed by the great physiologist of motor control, N.A. Bernstein. One of the most widely used and commonly accepted descriptions proposes a classification that includes basic CA components, namely: kinaesthetic differentiation, rhythmic ability, spatial orientation, complex motor reaction, balance ability and agility. Research findings have shown that maximal speed and speed-strength variables largely affect the manifestation of basic CA in children and adolescents.

The available findings provide evidence that basic CA, with the exception of spatial orientation have moderate to low genetic control and, therefore, are sufficiently trainable. Moreover, the rate of coordinative improvement, i.e. learnability, is less dependent on hereditary factors than CA themselves and, therefore, are sufficiently trainable (Lyalh, 2006). This fact supports the necessity of early coordination training, creating prerequisites for further successful formation of techno-tactical mastery. Furthermore, high learnability can be viewed as an earlier precursor of athletic giftedness. In addition, significant relationships have been revealed between basic CA and speed-strength variables in children and adolescents, whereas estimates of endurance and flexibility have had low and non-significant influence. Investigations of natural trends in the development of coordination competence have revealed a sensitive period of CA between ages 7-10 years. During this period, appropriate stimulation of CA using various athletic activities is strongly recommended. It was also established that the inclusion of coordination programs into the preparation of high-performance athletes produces a distinct stimulatory impact on both the fitness and technical components of athletic preparedness.

Purposeful coordination training presupposes realization of several principles related to the compilation of preparation programs for improvement of coordination competence and sport-specific preparedness in youth and adult high-performance athletes. These principles postulate that coordination training is an indispensable part of the whole preparation system (1), stimulation of basic CA should be integrated into technical preparation (2), coordination programs should accentuate individual strengths and properties of athletes (3), they should be closely connected with conditioning training (4), and the monitoring of basic CA should be part of the entire preparation system (5). Three principal approaches can be realized in the development of basic athletic CA, namely:

- Complex concurrent enhancement of many CA within sport-specific, techno-tactical preparation

- Accentuated training stimulation of properly selected CA affecting a specific athletic activity

- Realization of prospective coordination programs within long-term athletic preparation

In addition, there are proposed, generalized positions related to the content and particularities of coordination training during different stages of multiyear athletic preparation and several rules for the selection and compilation of coordination exercises.

Part 2 - Evaluation and development of Athletic Coordination Abilities

The second part of this book comprises the description and consideration of practical tools for evaluation and purposeful development of CA in athletes of various ages and athletic competence using appropriate exercises and tasks. The examples of exercises are clustered according to the previously considered basic CA and voluntary relaxation of muscles.

Chapter 5 - Evaluation and development of kinaesthetic differentiation

Kinaesthetic differentiation is the ability to differentiate spatial, temporal and strength characteristics of movements; this highly contributes to the construction and perfection of various motor skills. Correspondingly, its evaluation and enhancement is traditionally the focus of practical efforts, which are considered below.

5.1. Evaluation of kinaesthetic differentiation

Evaluation of kinaesthetic differentiation has been widely considered and described (Meinel and Schnabel, 1998; Belej and Junger, 2006; Lyakh, 2006). A number of motor trials, such as the following, have been proposed and validated:
- Measurement of accuracy of angular and linear arm and leg displacement (Figure 11);
- Measurement of accuracy of hand grip strength on a dynamometer with force application equal to 25, 50 and 75% of maximum effort; permissible error should be within 3%;
- Reproduction of time intervals of 0.3, 0.7 and 1.2s with a stopwatch;
- Backward medicine ball throw to target (1m diameter circle on the wall, behind the athlete) from a distance of 2m;
- Rolling a ball, pushing it with an arm for a 6m distance, estimating accuracy;
- Rolling a ball, kicking it a 6m distance, estimating accuracy;
- Standing long jump for a distance equal to 50% of maximal performance;
- Drop jump from a 90cm box to a target (horizontal line) on the floor; permissible error should be about 3-5cm.

In addition, a computerized test of kinaesthetic differentiation is widely used based on the Toshiba Satellite R15 program (Schuhfriegd, 1996).

Basic approaches directed toward improvement of this ability can be realized using two options: 1) Execution of exercises demanding accuracy in reproduction of several characteristics of movement (temporal, spatial or force application); 2) Execution of exercises demanding voluntary control during the entire motor task.

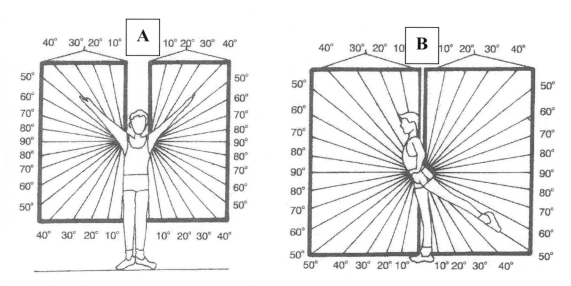

Figure 11. Reproduction of angular displacement of arms (A) and leg (B) using external marks

The first approach can be employed in relatively simple movements of the arms, legs, or whole body. The second approach can be utilized in more complex actions such as ball throwing, jumps, etc. During performance of these exercises, the athletes are requested to evaluate the accuracy of movement reproduction; this self-estimation is matched with the objective evaluation of the coach. After a number of repetitions, performance accuracy increases and the ability to differentiate movements is enhanced.

Exercises demanding accuracy of movement reproduction are associated with a certain difficulty for trainees. The method of "contrast motor tasks" has been elaborated to facilitate the process of coordination training. This method presupposes the sequencing of certain tasks with largely different movement variables. For instance: basketball shooting from distances of 4 and 6m; passing the ball in soccer from distances of 15 and 25m; broad jumping a maximal distance and half the distance, etc. In exercises for more qualified athletes, the contrast of external conditions can be reduced and the demands of movement differentiation will be higher.

Another approach is termed the "method of near motor tasks" that presupposes performance of sequenced attempts with relatively small differences in external conditions. Examples of such combinations are: reproduction of angular arm positions equal to 70, 80 and 90 degrees, basketball shooting from distances of 4 and 4.2m, shooting at a soccer goal from distances of 10.5, 11 and 11.5m, etc. This ability to accommodate movement in accordance with small differences of external conditions demands increased proprioceptive sensitivity and higher cognitive input. As a result, the athletes acquire an enhanced "sense of the ball," "sense of javelin," "sense of the water," etc.

5.2. Examples of exercises for children 7-10 years of age

This age generally corresponds to the initial or preliminary athletic preparation in several sports. However, the described exercises can also be recommended for older novices. The offered exercises exploit usual equipment; in many cases, the marking of training facilities using external visual orientation provides sufficient performance control (Table 15).

Table 15. Typical exercises for the development of kinaesthetic differentiation of 7-10 year old children

No	Exercise description	Comments
1	Standing in front of wall, the athlete raises two arms at sides to the horizontal position (a); 10 degrees lower (b); 10 degrees higher (c) etc.	Behind the athlete, appropriate visual marks of range of motion should be indicated. Performance control is required
2	Standing sideways to wall, the athlete raises straight leg to the horizontal position (a); 10 degrees lower (b); 10 degrees higher (c) etc.	The same
3	Standing sideways to wall, the athlete moves straight leg back to 10 degrees (a); to 20 degrees (b); to 30 degrees (c)	The same
4	Execution of squat from standing position (a); semi-squat (b); squat with raising arms forward to the horizontal position (c) etc.	Squat is performed to 90 degrees in knee joints; semi-squat – until 120 degrees. Execution with and without visual control
5	Execution of lunge forward with full range of motion (a); with half range of motion (b); combined with raising arms forward to the horizontal position (c) etc.	Full and half ROM lunge should be indicated on the floor by appropriate marks. Execution should be done with and without visual control.
6	Execution of lunge sideways with full and half range of motion and combined with arm movements	The same
7	In hanging position raising, two legs up to 90, 70 degrees, etc.	Range of motion is controlling by coach
8	Bending the body in standing position until 70, 90 and 120 degrees	Execution can be combined with additional arm movements
9	Walking in place with additional arm movements	Symmetrical and asymmetrical arm movements can be done with visual control of accuracy
10	Serial throwing of a ball to heights of 0.5, 1 and 1.5m in a standing position	Performance accuracy should be controlled by coach
11	The same exercise, throwing with one arm	The same
12	Serial jumps forward and back to distances of 20, 30 and 40cm	The jump's length should be indicated on floor by lines or sticks
13	Throwing the ball to target (hoops) from distances of 3, 4 and 5m	The targets are placed on the floor
14	The same exercise, throwing with one arm	Dominant and non-dominant arm should be sequenced
15	Passing the ball to a partner from different distances	Pass distance can be changed during the series
16	Basketball dribbling, changing the height of ball rebound	Rebound changing can be planned within one task or in subsequent attempts

A number of exercises (1-3) presuppose the execution of arm and/or leg movements with a predetermined range of motion using external orientation for visual control of performance accuracy. The initial attempts allow the trainees to familiarize with the motor task and activate proprioceptive feedback. The subsequent attempts, performed without vision, demand utilization of proprioceptive signaling. In addition, such exercises positively affect motor memory, which is also part of kinesthetic differentiation. Regular cues from the coach largely contribute to the acquisition of motor skills of movement regulation.

Similar demands are realized in exercises with squats and lunges (4-6), which presuppose self-estimation and regulation of range of motion in lower body activities. It is worth noting that these exercises are widely used in the fitness programs of youth athletes. Insertion of coordination demands enriches the fitness program and provides a conjugate effect in development of both conditioning and coordination abilities. This also relates to the leg-raising exercise in a hanging position, which is associated with tonic contraction of large muscle groups of the body (7th exercise). Similarly, bending the body in a standing position with a predetermined range of motion produces both a conditioning and neuro-regulatory impact (8th exercise).

Walking in place with additional arm movements provides sufficient freedom for a creative coach who can offer various combinations of symmetrical and asymmetrical movements, synchronized with the rhythm of steps (9th exercise). This exercise can be simply modified according to jogging or serial jumping. In any case, reproduction of precise arm movements during concomitant activity produces a desirable effect on the coordination competence of young athletes.

Repeated throwing of a ball to a predetermined height can be performed at low, medium and high tempos in standing and sitting positions (10th and 11th exercises). Special attention should be given to the accuracy of throws and catching of the ball. Additional modification of this exercise presupposes the execution of serial throwing while changing the height within one series. In this case, the trainee should regulate force application from a low to a medium and higher level. Similarly, serial jumps with a predetermined length demand accurate differentiation of take-off and appropriate cognitive efforts (12th exercise).

Throwing the ball to a target can be performed using different, predetermined ball trajectories (13th and 14th exercises). Execution of this exercise by one arm produces additional accentuated demands for the non-dominant arm, aiming to activate its proprioceptive control and reinforce motor skill transfer onto the dominant arm.

Passing the ball to a partner can be done with two and/or one arm, changing the pass distance within one task and/or in subsequent attempts (15th exercise). This exercise can be performed in a standing position or during pre-programmed jogging.

Basketball dribbling changing the height of the ball rebound is also associated with variations of movement rate (16th exercise). Dribbling can be performed moving forward, backward and sideways, individually or in a small group.

Evidentially, the execution of the above exercises requires a high amount of mental concentration from the athletes and, therefore, can mostly be planned for the initial part of workout. Several exercises can be recommended for independent home performance while using a mirror.

5.3. Examples of exercises for children 11-14 years of age

More matured children usually have larger motor experience and a wider range of various motor skills. Correspondingly, prescription of typical coordination exercises for this category includes motor tasks of higher complexity, demanding more pronounced muscular efforts (Table 16).

Table 16. Typical exercises for development of kinaesthetic differentiation of 11-14 year old children

No	Exercise description	Comments
1	Raising two arms symmetrically and asymmetrically to a predetermined angular position	This drill can be done in place or while walking and/or jogging, varying the movement's rate
2	Serial squats and/or semi-squats with predetermined arm raising	Squats and semi-squats can be done within one task or during separate tasks
3	Jumps from a kneeling position up to two legs (a) or to one leg (b)	This drill can be combined with body rotation to 90 or 180 degrees
4	Serial throwing of a heavy ball to heights of 1, 1.5, and 2m in standing or sitting positions	Throw height and catching accuracy should be controlled by coach
5	Passing a heavy ball to one or two partners from distances of 3, 4 and 5m	Accuracy of throwing and catching should be controlled by coach
6	Throwing and catching a stick with a partner	Can be done with two arms or one arm
7	Throwing a stick to a partner while simultaneously catching a second stick from the partner	Throwing frequency varies from low to medium
8	Lifting a barbell to knee height, to the hips, to the chest, to the shoulders	The weight of the barbell varies from light to medium. Lifts' accuracy should be controlled
9	Throwing a medicine ball to a target from different distances (Figure 12)	This drill can be done from a standing or sitting position
10	Standing long jump to a predetermined distance such as 1, 1.2, and/or 1.5m	Jumps can be done with and without visual control of jump's length
11	Single and serial body rolls forward and backward	Accuracy and reproduction of body rolls should be controlled
12	Passing of two balls with a partner or in a small group from different distances (Figure 13)	Can be done standing in place or while walking or jogging at a low or medium tempo
13	Rolling a ball to partners in small groups with arms and/or legs	Rolling speed and accuracy should be controlled
14	Throwing a tennis ball at the wall and catching it during rebound	Throw distance varies from small (2-3m) to medium (4-5 m)
15	Basketball dribbling with dominant and non-dominant arm changing the height of ball rebound	Rebound changes can be planned within one task or in subsequent attempts

The 1st exercise offers many variations of symmetrical and asymmetrical arm movements, reproducing various angular positions using visual and proprioceptive control. These motor tasks can be combined with walking and/or jogging, which provide an automatized background of general physical activity. Diversified arm movements stimulate voluntary proprioceptive control and short-term motor memory. Similarly, serial squats and/or semi-squats (2nd exercise) can serve as a physical background for superimposed, predetermined accurate arm movements.

Jumps from a kneeling to a standing position demand highly coordinated efforts of the lower body muscles that enhance agonist-antagonist co-activation (3rd exercise). Additional body rotation after the take-off increases the complexity of the drill and makes it more attractive.

Serial throwing of a medicine ball to different predetermined heights produces a valuable impact on the ability to regulate force application in accordance with external demands (4th exercise). An additional effect of this drill is associated with stimulation of strength endurance. A similar conjugate effect is produced by repeated passing of a heavy ball to partners from varied distances (5th exercise). In this case, the ability to regulate force application receives proper stimulation.

Passing a stick to a partner demands accuracy of the stick's orientation during throwing and precise coordination of arm muscles during the catch (6th exercise). A number of repetitions lead to partial automatization of a skill although high mental concentration remains important. The complexity of this exercise can be largely increased during simultaneous throws and counter-throws of two sticks by two partners (7th exercise). Such modification requires proper regulation of spatial, temporal and force variables in serial movements.

Lifting a barbell to a predetermined height produces a conjugate effect on kinaesthetic differentiation and strength endurance (8th exercise). Of course, the weight of barbell should correspond to the fitness level of the trainees and must not be excessive. Variations of the lift's height enrich proprioceptive input in motor coordination and lead to more conscious execution. After a number of repetitions, this exercise can be performed with restricted visual control and the importance of muscular sensations will be emphasized.

Throwing a heavy ball to a target can be done from short distances (3-4m), accentuating demands to accuracy, and from longer distances (6-7m), accentuating demands to force application (9th exercise, Figure 12). Both versions make sense and the best solution is to utilize a combination of the two. The execution of throws can be done forward or backward and in standing and/or sitting positions; this increases the diversity and desirability of the training program.

Standing long jumps to predetermined distances should be initially performed with visual control using appropriate marks on the floor (10th exercise). After a number of repetitions, visual control can be excluded and trainees are demanded to mobilize proprioceptive control and motor memory. Variations of jump distances, such as 1, 1.2, and 1.5m, diversify the program and increase the complexity of the motor task.

Figure 12. Throwing the medicine ball to a target from different distances

Execution of body rolls forward and backward presupposes preliminary acquisition of the motor skills that are usually familiar to 12-14 year old children (11th exercise). Therefore, execution of single rolls is not associated with particular difficulty. However, execution of repeated rolls demands more accentuated concentration and focus on uninterrupted, continuous performance.

Passing of two balls with a partner demands adequate and precise force differentiation (12th exercise, Figure 13). This demand is particularly accentuated while passing the ball to close and distantly located partners. The tempo variation allows for reinforcement of the complexity of the motor task.

Figure 13. Passing of two balls with partner

Similarly, rolling a ball to partners in small groups with the arms and/or legs (13th exercise) presupposes appropriate regulation of the direction and magnitude of force application.

Throwing a tennis ball against a wall and catching it during rebound is a highly demanding and attractive individual exercise (14th exercise). Rational ball trajectory causes its appropriate rebound and makes catching the ball possible. This exercise is also suitable for individual home preparation.

Basketball dribbling with the dominant and non-dominant arm is a widely used exercise. However, insertion of the additional demand associated with changing the height of the ball's rebound largely increases its coordination complexity (15th exercise). This exercise can be performed moving forward, backward and sideways. Notably, the involvement of the non-dominant arm makes sense for representatives of various sports with the aim of positive skill transfer to the dominant arm.

5.4. Examples of exercises for 15-19 year old athletes

The ages of 15-19 years generally correspond to a stage of advanced specialized preparation in many sport activities such as ball games, combat, power, endurance sports, and track and field. The selection of typical exercises introduces more advanced versions, where the level of complexity is reasonably higher than previously (Table 17).

Table 17. Typical exercises for the development of kinaesthetic differentiation in 15-19 year old athletes

No	Exercise description	Comments
1	Symmetrical and asymmetrical movements of arms in a standing position, during walking and/or jogging	Movement complexity and frequency varies within session from low to high
2	Lifting a barbell in standing position with two arms to chest (a), with body rotation (b), with jump (c)	Lift's height should be predetermined. It can be changed within one task or in separate, subsequent tasks
3	Serial jumps to a predetermined distance of 0.5, 1 or 1.5m	Jumps' route can be marked by hoops, lines, or sticks
4	Serial jumps throwing a medicine ball 0.5m high during each jump	Throws and catches should be done with two arms
5	Serial throws of a medicine ball forward, backward and sideways to a partner	Throws' distance and frequency are changed within one task or in separate, subsequent tasks
6	Jumps onto a bench forward and back (a), with body rotation to 90 (b) and 180 (c) degrees	Jumps' and rotation accuracy should be controlled
7	Walking on the hands when the legs are supported by a partner	Length and frequency of "steps" increase within one task and/or in subsequent tasks
8	Rope skipping, changing the height and frequency of skips	The contrast tasks presuppose performance with high rebound and low frequency, and with small rebound and high frequency
9	Serial execution of body rolls with longer and shorter body displacement	Accuracy of body rolls and length of the body displacement should be controlled
10	Single-leg long jumps after a 3-5 stride take-off run for maximal distance (a), 20cm closer (b), 40cm closer (c)	Predetermined jump length can be marked by line or stick. Attempts are performed with and without visual control
11	Execution of 10-20m sprint bouts with a maximal and predetermined speed	Speed variations are controlled measuring performance time
12	Dribbling of two balls with two hands forward, backward and sideways (Figure 14)	Height of rebound, frequency and moving direction can be changed within one task
13	Passing of two balls in small groups with one or two arms from different distances	Exercise can be done standing in place, while walking or jogging in low, medium or high tempo
14	Shooting a ball to a target with an arm or leg without visual control	Preliminary attempt is done with vision; afterwards – based on motor memory

The 1st exercise presents a typical combination of various arm movements during it's execution in a standing position, during walking and jogging. The basic coordination demands of this exercise are associated with high reproduction of given movements despite the changing of external conditions (i.e. standing, walking and jogging). This motor task requires high mental concentration and motor memory.

Lifting a weight with a preplanned amplitude (2nd exercise) demands accentuated proprioceptive control. Insertion of additional tasks such as concomitant body rotation or a jump in the final phase of lifting increases the complexity of this exercise as well as activation of additional muscle groups.

Serial jumps for predetermined distances demand precise force application during take-off and its high reproduction during successive jumps (3rd exercise). This drill can clearly demonstrate and stimulate the ability to differentiate muscular efforts in lower body activity.

Serial jumps while throwing a medicine ball to a height of 0.5m demands precise force application and its high reproduction during successive throws (4th exercise). The jumps can be performed in place or with forward displacement.

Serial throws of a medicine ball with various modifications require appropriate force regulation and catching accuracy from a partner (5th exercise). Changing the throwing distance and frequency increases coordination complexity and allows for reinforcement of the conditioning effect directed toward strength endurance. Similarly, serial jumps onto a bench with and without body rotation produce a multilateral effect on effort regulation of the lower body and postural muscles (6th exercise). A conjugate effect on coordination and fitness should be reasonably expected.

Walking on the hands while the legs are supported by a partner can be performed with "step" regulation, from short to longer, or with a changing frequency of movements (7th exercise). This exercise can be organized as a competition between athletes. In this case, a "speed trial" presupposes rational interaction between the "racer" and the "supporter," who assists in the forward displacement of the couple. Correspondingly, this coordination program includes "partnership" and attraction.

Rope skipping is a widely popular exercise in various sports. Additional tasks such as changing the height and frequency of skips and body rotations diversify the coordination program and increase workload (8th exercise). Similarly, body rolls are popular and widely used in fitness programs. Serial body rolls can consist of 3-4 repetitions with preprogrammed longer and shorter body displacement (9th exercise). In both cases, total body displacement should be indicated and used for follow up in subsequent attempts.

The next drill is a single-leg long jump, which should be done after a 3-5 stride take-off run (10th exercise). The first trial should be done for maximal distance. Subsequent attempts should be done aiming for distances that are 20 and 40cm shorter using a visual mark and without visual control. Performance accuracy should be judged.

Execution of sprint bouts should be performed with the goal of refining the sense of speed at distances of 10-20m. (11th exercise). The 1st attempt should be done with maximal effort. 2-3 subsequent trials should be done with a predetermined speed reduction, increasing performance time by 0.2-0.4s. As a result, the athletes should enhance their speed sensation.

Dribbling of two balls with two hands is a rather difficult coordination task (12th exercise, Figure 14). Changing the direction of body displacement, i.e. forward, backward, and sideways, increases the complexity of the motor task. Additional demands, including changing the height of the ball rebound, increase the complexity and attraction of this exercise.

Figure 14. Dribbling of two balls with two hands

Passing of two balls in small groups (3-4 athletes) with one or two arms can be done changing the distances between partners. This drill can be done standing in place initially; afterwards, while walking or jogging at slow to medium tempos (13th exercise).

Shooting a ball to a target (2m diameter circle on the wall) with an arm or leg without visual control can be done from distances of 3-5m (14th exercise). Initial attempts should be done with vision; subsequent attempts, without vision. Performance accuracy should be judged.

Chapter 6 - Evaluation and development of spatial orientation

The general principal approach to the development and perfection of spatial abilities presupposes systematic utilization of purposeful exercises that demand accurate and rapid orientation in space. Very often, these exercises include additional demands to kinaesthetic differentiation, agility and several sport-specific skills. These additional demands increase the complexity of exercises and their effect on the coordination competence of trainees.

6.1. Evaluation of spatial orientation

Evaluation of the spatial orientation of athletes presupposes the determination of accuracy and speed of performance in specially designed motor tasks. For this purpose, several standardized motor tests have been proposed and verified (Meinel and Schnabel, 1998; Belej and Junger, 2006; Lyakh,2006; Notarnicola et al., 2014). As a result, the following tests have become widely used and popular in research and practice. Namely:

3. The athlete throws a tennis ball backwards, without vision, aiming to hit a medicine ball placed 2m behind the athlete on the floor; the throw's accuracy is judged;
4. The athlete rolls three balls using both arms and legs along an 11m slalom route with four obstacles (vaulting boxes); performance time is estimated;
5. 3×3m shuttle run to an arbitrarily called numbered ball among 5 numbered balls placed at a distance of 1.5m from each other; performance time is estimated (Figure 15);
6. A blindfolded athlete performs a series of lateral and forward steps and then turns following the command of the coach and returns to the starting point; performance accuracy is judged;
7. A "2D Visualization" computerized test that requires reconstruction of a spatial figure using the appropriate spatial elements (Schuhfriegd, 1996).

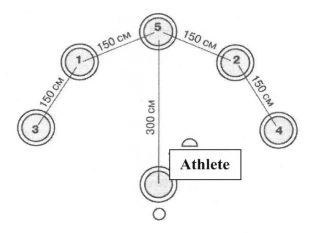

Figure 15. 3×3m shuttle run to arbitrarily called numbered balls (P. Hirtz, 1985)
The coach calls out the number of the ball; an athlete runs to that numbered ball, touches it, and runs back and touches the central ball. Right then, the coach calls out another number and the athlete runs to touch it. The total time of three runs is measured. Performance times equal to 7.8s for boys and 8.0s for girls indicate a high level in 14 year old athletes

The testing practice presupposes that athletes have preliminary familiarity with the trial's protocol, execution of one-two preliminary attempts, and a final performance. Usually, relatively simple equipment is used in these examinations, although the use of video registration is recommended.

6.2. Examples of exercises for 7-10 year old children

Table 18 introduces a number of typical exercises that can be recommended for the development of spatial orientation in 7-10 year old children. It is worth noting that in most sports, these drills form the basic platform for general coordination competence, whereas in highly coordinated esthetic sports (i.e. gymnastics, figure skating, etc.) these drills should be accomplished within the sport-specific program.

Table 18. Typical exercises for the development of spatial orientation in 7-10 year old children

No	Exercise description	Comments
1	In supine lying position, raising of both arms upward symmetrically and asymmetrically	Spatial orientation of arms should be controlled
2	In supine lying position, raising of both legs upward symmetrically and asymmetrically	Spatial orientation of legs should be controlled
3	In prone lying position, execution of body turn while raising arms and/or legs upward symmetrically and asymmetrically	Spatial orientation of arms and legs should be controlled
4	Execution of 3 steps forward, turn and 3 steps backward with and without visual control	Performance accuracy is controlled
5	Execution of 3 jumps forward, turn and 3 jumps backward with and without visual control	Jumps' length should be 30-50cm; jumps' tempo varies from low to medium
6	Jogging with crawls under a beam or through a barrier	Appropriate precautions to prevent injuries are necessary
7	Serial jumps to hoops on floor with one and/or two legs	Jumps' length is 40-70cm; jumps' tempo varies for 10-20m from low to medium
8	The same drill with body rotations to 90 degrees	Forward direction and accuracy of athlete displacement is controlled
9	Backward walking and running along a gymnastics bench	Speed and accuracy of athlete's displacement is controlled
10	Standing jump with predetermined body turns to 90, 180 and 270 degrees	The turns' accuracy is controlled
11	The same drill with backward body displacement	Accuracy of turns and body displacement are controlled
12	Execution of 3 body rolls forward and 3 body rolls backward with and without vision	Direction of body displacement is controlled
13	Drop jump from a 70cm box with a precise landing in a hoop	Landing accuracy is controlled

The initial three exercises are directed to adapt trainees to adequate perception of spatial position of various body links. Exercising in a lying position is associated with modified apprehension of space and spatial variables. Execution of symmetrical and asymmetrical movements in varied conditions enriches the motor experience of children in modified spatial conditions.

Execution of the 4th and 5th exercises with and without visual control offer special demands to space perception. In addition, these drills demand mobilization of motor memory during the task performance without vision. The initial attempts should be performed under visual control; the subsequent performance without vision should provide valuable experience in comprehension and remembering of body sensations.

The 6th exercise requires adequate spatial orientation while overcoming certain obstacles using predetermined behavioral strategies such as crawling under a beam or through a barrier. Such motor tasks presuppose the utilization of non-standardized motor skills and increase the attraction of the coordination program. Serial jumps to hoops on the floor (7th drill) demand manifestation of purposeful spatial behavior where each jump should be directed toward the appropriate targeted zone marked by a hoop. Preliminary familiarity with this exercise allows athletes to demonstrate efficient spatial orientation in subsequent attempts. Additional body turns during a jump's performance increases the complexity of the exercise and its demands to spatial organization (8th drill).

Backward walking and running along a gymnastic bench (9th drill) demand confident motor behavior in an unusual spatial situation. After preliminary familiarity with the motor task, children can demonstrate efficient performance in subsequent attempts and good spatial orientation during backward displacement.

A standing jump with a predetermined body turn is a highly demanding motor task. Whereas jumps with body rotation to 90 and 180 degrees demand mostly spatial orientation, a jump with body rotation to 270 degrees also presupposes mobilization of an explosive fitness component (10th and 11th exercises).

Execution of body rolls forward and backward (12th drill) are associated with accentuated spatial demands. An initial attempt should be done with visual control and subsequent attempts demand the involvement of spatial perception and motor memory. Similarly, the execution of drop jumps with a precise landing to a targeted area marked by a hoop emphasize demands to spatial orientation and neuromuscular regulation (13th drill).

6.3. Examples of exercises for 11-14 year old children

Selecting exercises for spatial orientation for more mature children includes more difficult tasks involving interaction with partners (Table 19).

Table 19. Typical exercises for development of spatial orientation in 11-14 year old children

No	Exercise description	Comments
1	In lying prone position, moving of arms aside symmetrically and asymmetrically	Spatial orientation of arms should be controlled
2	In lying prone position, raising of straight and/or bent legs upward symmetrically and asymmetrically	Spatial orientation of legs should be controlled
3	In lying supine position, throwing and catching a medicine ball at a height of 1m	Throws' height and catching accuracy should be controlled
4	The same exercise with a partner who catches the ball and throws it back	The throws' frequency can be increased
5	Two partners standing 3m apart throw balls upward and change positions to catch their partner's ball	The throws' height should be sufficient for changing position and catching the ball
6	Throw the ball upward and catch it after performance of a 180 degree body turn	The throw's height should be sufficient for performance of body turn
7	Body roll, body turn to 180 degrees and performance of a 2nd body roll	The athlete should obtain the same location that he was prior the 1st roll
8	Serial sideways jumps over a gymnastics bench with forward displacement	8-10 jumps can be performed
9	Backward running in a small group in a circle of about 20m	Spatial location of athletes within the group should be controlled
10	Drop jump from a 90cm box with precise landing in hoop	Landing accuracy is controlled
11	Throw a ball at the wall from a distance of 4m and catch it after rebound	Throw direction can be varied; the throw-catch tempo varies from low to medium
12	Dribbling a ball within a "corridor" for a distance of 12m with and without visual control	The "corridor" is marked with lines; its width is about 2m
13	Similar exercise with dribbling of a soccer ball with legs	The "corridor" is marked with lines; its width is about 3m
14	Jumps from a circle to another circle in different directions (a); jumps over the circles (b), jumps to circles with body rotation of 90 degrees (c)	Gymnastic hoops can be used for the circles. Three hoops are placed sequentially (Figure 16)

The arm and leg movements in a prone lying position are associated with additional difficulties in spatial orientation due to the specific body position and restricted visual control (1st and 2nd exercises). Similarly, throwing and catching a ball in a lying supine position demands higher spatial accuracy due to the inability to change body position and catch a distant ball (3rd exercise). The same exercise with a partner who stands in front of the lying trainee and catches the ball allows for an increase in the throws' tempo and to increase the metabolic demands of the motor task (4th exercise).

The 5th exercise requires more pronounced spatial perception and spatial interaction with a partner. Two athletes should throw their balls upward to a height of about 2m and change their location to catch their partner's ball. Of course, this more sophisticated task demands rational interaction between partners and high accuracy in their spatial behavior.

The 6th exercise offers a highly coordinated action with throwing a ball upward, rapidly performing a body turn of 180 degrees, and catching the falling ball. This motor task demands high mental concentration and, therefore, should be performed with sufficient intervals. Thus, the anticipated performance frequency varies from low to medium.

Execution of a body roll followed by a 180 degree turn and performance of a 2nd body roll assumes the athlete will return to their starting place (7th exercise). Coincidence of starting and ending places during performance of this task provides an indication of the rational spatial orientation of the athlete.

Serial sideways jumps over a gymnastics bench are associated with high metabolic demands (8th exercise), where forward displacement inserts additional conditions for spatial behavior. The jumps' length and frequency can be increased in subsequent attempts. Correspondingly, exercise intensity can vary from medium to high. Similarly, backward running in a circle of about 20m (9th exercise) combines the demands of conditioning training and spatial orientation.

Drop jumps from a box with landing to a targeted zone marked by hoop (10th exercise) presupposes execution of precise, spatially organized action. Visual control allows for sufficient accuracy, even in the initial attempt. Subsequent attempts can be performed with restricted vision based on the athlete's proprioceptive control.

Throwing a ball to the wall and catching it after rebound (11th exercise) can be practiced by changing the throws' trajectory, moving along the wall. The tempo of action can be reasonably increased during performance and in subsequent attempts.

Dribbling a ball within a "corridor" demands increased spatial and cognitive control (12th exercise). The initial attempts should be performed with vision whereas subsequent attempts can be done with restricted vision or without visual control. A similar exercise proposes the execution of soccer dribbling within a "corridor" (13th exercise). In both cases (basketball and soccer dribbling), rational spatial behavior is highly demanded.

The next drill (14th exercise) offers three variants. The first one requires spatial accuracy when jumping from a hoop to another hoop (a); the second one presupposes jumping over the hoops (b); the third task demands jumping to the hoops with body rotation (c). Correspondingly, the spatial complexity increases from the first to third version (Figure 16).

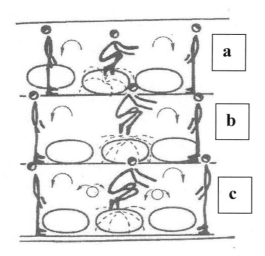

Figure 16. Jumps from a circle to another circle in different directions

6.4. Examples of exercises for 15-19 year old athletes

This category of athletes already has substantial experience of previous preparation and a relatively high level of athletic ambitions. Nevertheless, coordination training for spatial orientation remains important and the selection of exercises should correspond to their higher level of both athletic abilities and athletic ambitions (Table 20).

Table 20. Typical exercises for development of spatial orientation of 15-19 year old athletes

No	Exercise description	Comments
1	In lying prone position, execution of a body turn to supine position and raising of arms and legs symmetrically and asymmetrically	Spatial orientation of arms and legs should be controlled
2	In lying prone position, raising of straight and bent legs upward and to the side symmetrically and asymmetrically	Spatial orientation of legs should be controlled
3	In lying supine position, throwing and catching a medicine ball to a height of about 1.5m	Throws' height and catching accuracy should be controlled
4	Execution of the same exercise with a partner who catches the ball and throws it back	The throws' tempo increases from medium to high
5	Two partners standing 3m apart, each throw a ball upward, change positions and catch the partner's ball	The throws' height should be sufficient for changing position and catching the ball
6	The athlete throws a medicine ball upward, jumps with body rotation of 360 degrees and catches the ball	The throws' height should be sufficient for performance of the jump with body rotation prior to catching the ball
7	Execution of 3 body rolls and throwing of a medicine ball backward to a target on the wall	Target on the wall is a 2×2m square
8	Serial sideways jumps over a gymnastics bench with backward body displacement	10-12 jumps can be performed
9	Hanging on a high horizontal bar while executing body swings with a jump down to a targeted zone	Targeted zone on the floor is a 1×1m square. Landing accuracy is controlled
10	Running in a circle, jumping over low hurdles	6-8 hurdles should be placed in the route
11	From a handstand position, execution of forward and/or backward body roll	Handstand position can be maintained with support of partner
12	Drop jump from a 1m box with precise landing in a hoop	Landing accuracy is controlled
13	One partner throws a ball at the wall from a 4-5m distance, the 2nd partner catches the ball after rebound (Figure 17a)	Throw direction can be varied; the 2nd partner should anticipate the rebound direction
14	One partner throws a ball at the wall from a 4-5m distance, the 2nd partner catches the ball after rebound from floor (Figure 17b)	The place where the ball contacts the floor can be marked. The throwing and catching accuracy are controlled
15	Dribbling a ball within a 16m "corridor" with and without visual control	The "corridor" is marked with lines; its width is about 2m
16	A similar exercise with dribbling of a soccer ball with legs	The "corridor" is marked with lines; its width is about 3m

The first two exercises should be performed in a lying position and demand raising the arms and legs symmetrically and asymmetrically (1st exercise) and raising of straight and bent legs upward and to the side (2nd exercise). In both cases, execution of these elementary actions activates basic prerequisites of spatial orientation. Throwing and catching a medicine ball in the lying supine position is intended to stimulate spatial adaptation and increase accuracy of spatial manipulations (3rd exercise). Execution of a similar task with a partner (4th exercise) allows for a large increase in throwing frequency and reinforces the conditioning effect of this drill.

The 5th exercise was also recommended for the previous age category. More mature athletes should perform it with higher accuracy and rational interaction between partners. The 6th exercise presupposes throwing a medicine ball upward, combined with a 360 degree body rotation during a jump prior to catching the ball. Such jumping performance demands a highly accentuated neuromuscular effort. In critical cases, the body's rotation amplitude can be reduced to 180 degrees.

Execution of 3 body rolls (7th exercise) is associated with pronounced irritation of vestibular receptors. These signals aggravate the performance of accurate spatially oriented action (backward throws of a medicine ball to a targeted zone). Nevertheless, using a number of repetitions, the athletes will adapt to vestibular irritation and can achieve sufficiently precise performance, enhancing their spatial orientation.

Serial sideways jumps over a gymnastic bench demand distinct spatial accuracy and produce a pronounced impact on general fitness. Backward body displacement during serial jumps emphasizes demands to spatial precision and produces valuable input to improvement of coordination competence (8th exercise).

Execution of body swings hanging on a high horizontal bar is the initial phase of the 9th exercise. The final and most important phase of this drill is a downward jump with accurate landing within a targeted zone that is marked on the floor. Although the targeted zone is relatively large (1×1m square) a precise landing requires a sufficient level of spatial orientation.

Running in a circle while jumping over low hurdles requires manifestation of spatial orientation combined with appropriate visual control and skill plasticity (10th exercise). Running speed, height and number of hurdles allow for regulation of the workload.

Execution of body rolls forward and/or backward from a handstand position (11th exercise) are associated with accentuated manifestation of spatial orientation, taking into account difficulties in spatial perception and lack of experience in such motor tasks. However, repeated performances allow for substantial improvement in this ability and positively affect general coordination competence.

Drop jumps from a box presuppose a sufficient level of spatial perception for provision of a precise landing within a hoop located on the floor (12th exercise). In addition, such a drill provides favorable neuromuscular stimulation, which occurs during the amortization phase of the landing.

The next two exercises (13th and 14th), presuppose rational interaction between partners. The first partner should throw the ball at a wall accurately, providing an appropriate trajectory and the 2nd partner should catch the ball after rebound from the wall (Figure 17a) or from the floor (Figure 17b). In both cases, appropriate spatial accuracy is demanded from both partners.

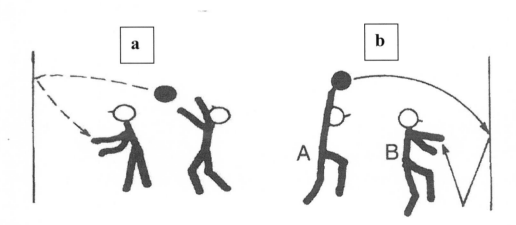

Figure 17. Throwing a ball at a wall with a partner catching it after rebound from the wall (a) and from floor (b)

The last two exercises (15th and 16th), offer execution of very familiar motor tasks such as basketball dribbling (15th exercise) and soccer dribbling (16th exercise). In both cases, the athletes should perform movements within a relatively narrow "corridor." Importantly, the initial attempts should be performed with visual control whereas subsequent trials should be done without vision. Execution of these attempts demands the manifestation of accentuated spatial orientation and motor memory.

Chapter 7 - Evaluation and development of body balance ability

Balance ability serves for control of spatial body position while maintaining its equilibrium and postural stability in static and dynamic conditions. Its manifestation embraces both aquatic and terrestrial sports and cannot be underestimated.

7.1. Evaluation of body balance ability

Evaluation and development of balance ability has traditionally been a focus of attention of sport science experts and coaches. A number of appropriate motor tests were proposed, verified and implemented in research and coaching practice for the examination of both static and dynamic body balance in youth and adult athletes. The most popular and practically acceptable tests are listed below:

8. Romberg test - maintenance of static balance during a one leg stance with closed eyes (Figure 18);
9. Maintenance of static balance during bipedal stance on a balance board as long as possible (until floor contact); maximum - 30s (Figure 19);
10. Walking forward and backward on the beam of upturned gymnastics benches;
11. Execution of four, full body turns on the beam of upturned gymnastics benches

Estimates for identification of a high level of body balance ability are presented below (Table 21).

Table 21. Estimates of high level balance ability based on several motor tests (seconds)
(based on Belej and Junger, 2006; Lyakh, 2006)

Age	Gender	Romberg test	Balancing on the balance board	Walking on the upturned bench	4 turns on the upturned bench
10	M	11.7	4.3	16.9	11
	F	9.8	3.3	20.1	12.5
14	M	21.3	3.6	12.7	10
	F	14.8	2.6	15.1	11.2
17	M	26.8	11.1	15.8	9,5
	F	19.6	4.2	16.6	10,3
20	M	18.2	12.2	12.5	9,4
	F	19.9	8.9	14.1	10,2

Figure 18. Maintenance of static balance on one leg during Romberg test

Figure 19. Maintenance of static balance standing on balance board

In laboratory conditions, the Biodex Balance System is widely used. This system contains a movable platform with registration of deviations of the center of gravity from the horizontal plane during single-leg and bipedal stances for a 30s time period (Arnold and Schmitz, 1998).

The majority of the exercises used for the development of balance ability (Tables 22-24) provide objective indicators of performance quality that can be used for monitoring during the preparation process.

7.2. Examples of exercises for 7-10 year old children

Children aged 7-10 years have a relatively low level of balance ability. Correspondingly, the selection of exercises are relatively simple and use readily available equipment (Table 22).

Table 22. Typical exercises for development of balance ability of 7-10 year old children

No	Exercise description	Comments
1	Maintenance of single-leg stance position with open and closed eyes	Duration of static body balance is controlled
2	Execution of various arm movements in a single-leg stance position	Arm movements should not disturb stance stability
3	Balancing while standing on medicine ball with and without visual control (Figure 20)	Combined with balancing movements of arms
4	Balancing of a stick that is placed in the palm of the hand	The stick's height (vertical position) should be maintained
5	Walking along the beam of an upturned gymnastics bench, forward and backward	This task is combined with balancing movements of arms
6	Walking along the beam of an upturned gymnastics bench overcoming obstacles	Medicine balls can be placed along the bench as obstacles
7	The same exercise combined with execution of squats and semi-squats	Squats and semi-squats are performed every 3-4 steps
8	Body turns on the beam of an upturned gymnastics bench	3-4 body turns should be performed to the left and right sides
9	Walking on tiptoes forward and backward along a gymnastics bench	Stable and balanced body position should be controlled
10	Execution of 3 body rolls followed by a jump to a single-leg stance position	Final jump can be performed with and/or without arm swing
11	Execution of lunge forward with a full range of motion maintaining balance in final position	Static balance should be maintained for 8-10s
12	Serial jumps on one leg with a pause between jumps	After each jump, single-leg position should be maintained for a 3s pause

The 1st exercise presupposes maintenance of a single-leg stance position with open eyes in the initial attempt and with closed eyes in subsequent attempts. The stance stability should be controlled by the coach; its duration should last about 30s or more. Additional arm movements increase the complexity of the motor task and can be reasonably included in the program (2nd exercise).

Maintaining body balance while standing on a medicine ball (3rd exercise) should be initially performed with visual control (Figure 20). After a number of repetitions, this motor task can be successfully performed without vision. In this case, proprioceptive control becomes the dominant function.

Figure 20. Balancing in a bipedal position standing on a medicine ball

Balancing of stick that is placed in the palm of the hand (4th exercise) is both an attractive and difficult motor task that demands high mental concentration and adjustment of the muscles of the entire body. The duration of stick balancing should increase with practice up to 30s.

Walking along the beam of an upturned gymnastics bench is a typical motor task for dynamic balance (5th exercise). The initial attempts presuppose forward displacement whereas subsequent trials should combine both forward and backward walking. The complexity of this exercise can be increased if the athletes have to overcome obstacles (medicine balls) placed on the route of the balanced walking (6th exercise) or if they execute additional movements such as squats and semi-squats during performance (7th exercise).

Body turns on the beam of an upturned gymnastics bench is one of the most difficult tasks of dynamic balance (8th exercise). The initial attempts can be performed with external support (coach, partner). Purposeful adaptation leads to formation of appropriate motor skills and the ability to perform 3-4 body turns to the left and right sides while increasing performance tempo.

One of the most popular dynamic balance exercises is walking on the tiptoes forward and backward (9th exercise). Moving along a gymnastics bench adds more complexity and attraction to this coordination drill. Combining forward and backward displacement in the same trial can be recommended.

Premature irritation of vestibular receptors produces substantial difficulties for body balance in the subsequent phase of a motor task. From this supposition, maintenance of body balance in a single-leg stance position after execution of 3 body rolls can be viewed as an original and highly demanding motor task (10th exercise).

Maintaining balance after execution of a forward lunge with full range of motion is associated with accentuated proprioceptive neuromuscular control and cognitive input (11th exercise). Similarly, maintenance of body balance in a pause between one-legged jumps is associated with pronounced neuromuscular control and mental concentration (12th exercise).

7.3. Examples of exercises for 11-14 year old children

The selection of exercises for children 11-14 years of age offers more difficult motor tasks including restriction or exclusion of visual control (Table 23).

Table 23. Typical exercises for development of balance ability of 11-14 year old children

No	Exercise description	Comments
1	Raising toes, standing on heels, maintaining body balance	This exercise should be performed with and without vision
2	In a single-leg stance, jump to the other leg while maintaining a balanced body position	This exercise can be done with and without vision
3	From a position sitting on the heels, jump, with arm swing, to a standing position	The balanced body position after the jump should be controlled
4	Maintenance of balance while standing on a medicine ball and rising onto the toes	Balanced standing on the toes should be maintained for 3-5s
5	Balancing of a stick that is placed in the palm of the hand while walking along a gymnastics bench (Figure 21)	The stick's vertical, balanced position should be maintained
6	Maintaining balance when a 2-3kg medicine ball is placed on the head while standing and executing semi-squats (Figure 22)	This drill can be combined with balancing movements of the arms
7	Walking with short steps on the toes along the beam of an upturned gymnastics bench, forward and backward	This drill can be combined with balancing movements of the arms
8	Execution of 3 body turns on the beam of an upturned gymnastics bench	Duration of performance should be controlled
9	Execution of 3 body rolls followed by walking on the beam of an upturned gymnastics bench	Stable body position while walking is controlled
10	Mutual body turn of two partners standing on a gymnastics bench	Performing a mutual body turn, the partners should assist each other
11	Execution of a handstand with the head on a medicine ball (Figure 23)	Duration of handstand should be about 30s
12	Hanging on a high horizontal bar, the athlete performs body swings followed by a jump downwards to a single-leg body position	Stable and balanced single-leg body position should be controlled

The first exercise challenges the maintenance of body balance in a bipedal stance while raising the toes and standing on the heels. This relatively simple coordination drill can be initially performed with vision and afterwards without visual control. The 2nd exercise proposes jump performance from a single-leg stance to the opposite leg while maintaining a balanced body position for 3-5s. After a couple of repetitions, this task can be performed without visual control.

The 3rd exercise demands a combination of balance ability with explosive efforts of the lower body muscles. The athlete should jump, using arm swing, from a sitting position on the heels to a standing position and maintaining the balanced stance position for 3-5s.

The 4th exercise demands the maintenance of balanced standing on a medicine ball while periodically raising onto the toes. Initial attempts can be done with external support; subsequent attempts should be done independently.

The 5th exercise presupposes walking along a gymnastics bench while balancing a stick that is placed in the palm of the hand (Figure 21). This relatively difficult motor task demands the rational adjustment of the arm's and postural body muscles and can be successfully fulfilled after a couple of preliminary attempts.

Figure 21. Balancing of stick while walking along a gymnastics bench

The 6th exercise proposes balancing while standing with a medicine ball placed on the head of the athlete. After a couple of preliminary attempts, the athlete is required to perform slow semi-squats with a low frequency (Figure 22).

Figure 22. Balancing in standing position when a medicine ball is placed on the head

The 7th exercise presupposes walking forward and backward with short steps on the toes along the beam of an upturned gymnastics bench. The steps' length and frequency should be individually adapted to athlete's desire. The next drill proposes the execution of 3 body turns on the beam of an upturned gymnastics bench (8th exercise). This balance task is the most difficult among this group, however, following a number of repetitions, the athletes can obtain a rational and stable performance.

Very often, sport practice demands the manifestation of balance ability immediately after irritation of vestibular receptors. Correspondingly, walking on the beam of an upturned gymnastic bench after the execution of 3 body rolls has distinct practical application (9th exercise).

The next motor task presupposes the rational interaction of two partners, who should perform a mutual body turn while standing on a gymnastic bench (10th exercise). This task requires individual creativity and a predisposition to rational partnership during an unusual coordination action.

A handstand while keeping the head on a medicine ball is usually a novel motor task for the majority of the athletic population (11th exercise). Correspondingly, the initial attempts can be done with external support, whereas subsequent attempts can be fulfilled independently. The required duration of the handstand varies between 15-20s (Figure 23).

Figure 23. Standing on the arms while the head is placed on a medicine ball

The last exercise in this group should be performed while hanging on a high horizontal bar and includes performing of a number of body swings followed by a jump downwards to a single-leg body position (12th exercise). Maintaining a balanced, one-legged position after landing is associated with distinct difficulty and involvement of external support during the initial attempts is recommended.

7.4. Examples of exercises for 15-19 year old athletes

The athletes of this age category are usually more experienced in various body balance activities and familiar with numerous situations where body equilibrium must be controlled. Correspondingly, the offered selection of balance exercises includes motor tasks of higher complexity. Of course, 15-19 year old athletes usually obtain a relatively high level of athletic mastery in their selected sports. Nevertheless, the offered exercises for balance ability provide a valuable contribution to coordination competence of athletes from different sports (Table 24).

Table 24. Typical exercises for development of balance ability in 15-19 year old athletes

No	Exercise description	Comments
1	Walking and jogging with short steps on the beam of an upturned gymnastics bench	This drill can be combined with balancing movements of the arms
2	Walking backward on the beam of an upturned gymnastics bench	This drill can be combined with balancing movements of the arms
3	Walking and jogging while holding a medicine ball on the head (Figure 22)	Stable and balanced ball position should be controlled
4	Walking along a gymnastics bench while throwing and catching a ball (upward) after every two steps	Throws' height is about 1m; balanced body position during throw and catch is controlled
5	Execution of various arm movements while standing on a medicine ball	Stable and balanced body position should be controlled
6	Execution of 4 body turns on the beam of an upturned gymnastics bench	Duration of performance should be controlled
7	Serial jumps on one leg combined with swings of another leg	Jumps' tempo varies from low to medium
8	Execution of handstand with the head on a medicine ball (Figure 23)	Vertical balanced body position should be controlled
9	Two partners kneeling face-to-face, holding a ball between their foreheads; they should stand up while holding the ball (Figure 24)	The partners interact, maintaining a mutual, balanced position
10	Moving on all fours, the athlete pushes a ball with their head along a gymnastics bench (Figure 25)	Accurate ball pushing is determined by its smooth and stable rolling
11	Execution of handstand with and without the support of a partner	Athlete should try to hold handstand independently
12	Walking on the hands while a partner supports the legs	Vertical balanced body position should be controlled

The 1st exercise proposes walking and jogging with short steps on the beam of an upturned gymnastics bench. Although this drill is familiar for trainees, displacement with jogging is associated with more pronounced demands for dynamic balance regulation. Similarly, backward walking on the beam of an upturned gymnastics bench requires activation of visual and proprioceptive neuromuscular control (2nd exercise).

Holding a medicine ball on the head demands manifestation of static body balance whereas execution of this motor task while walking or jogging requires dynamic balance and becomes a drill of higher complexity (3rd exercise). Movement rate during displacement varies from low to medium.

Additional motor tasks such as throwing a ball upward and catching it while walking along a gymnastics bench definitely increases the complexity and attraction of balance training (4th exercise). However, 15-19 year old athletes usually succeed with this drill after a couple of attempts.

The execution of various arm movements while standing on a medicine ball is associated with additional demands to dynamic balance and requires a couple of preliminary attempts with external control (5th exercise). Symmetrical and asymmetrical arm movements increase the complexity and attraction of the practiced exercises. The next exercise proposes execution of 4 body turns on the beam of an upturned gymnastics bench (6th exercise). This drill also serves for evaluation of dynamic balance ability; therefore, measurement of performance time is strongly recommended.

The 7th exercise presupposes execution of serial jumps on one leg combined with swings of the other leg. This dynamic balance exercise can be performed with balancing arm movements or while keeping the hands on the waist.

Maintenance of balance in a handstand position (8th exercise, Figure 23) is associated with specific spatial perception and accentuated proprioceptive control. The initial attempts can be done with external assistance, whereas subsequent performances can be done independently and should last about 20s.

The 9th exercise presupposes interaction of two partners, who kneel face-to-face while holding a ball between their foreheads. The partners should stand up while holding the ball and maintaining a balanced position (Figure 24). In subsequent attempts, the athletes can lower their body positions back to kneeling.

Figure 24. Rising up of two partners holding a ball between their foreheads

The 10th exercise proposes an athlete move on all fours along a gymnastics bench while pushing a ball with their head (Figure 25). This unusual exercise demands accurate body-link displacement to prevent the ball from falling and to maintain a balanced body position.

Figure 25. Pushing a ball with the head while moving along a gymnastics bench on all fours

The 11th exercise proposes the execution of a handstand that is usually not possible for the majority of athletes. Correspondingly, this drill should be done with external support, with a partner or coach assisting in the maintenance of a balanced, vertical body position for 15-20s. Similarly, the 12th exercise also demands performance in a handstand position; the athlete should perform a number of steps with the arms (walking on the hands) while a partner supports his/her legs, maintaining a balanced, vertical body position.

Chapter 8 - Evaluation and development of rhythmic ability

The importance of rhythmic ability cannot be underestimated. It is responsible for the adjustment and reproduction of temporal rhythm and movement rates of motor performance. It can be considered an indispensable part of purposeful coordination training for any sport.

8.1. Evaluation of rhythmic ability

Evaluation of rhythmic ability presupposes the use of appropriate motor tests and sport-specific trials. A number of specialized tests have been approved for evaluating rhythmic abilities in athletes (Hirtz, 1985; Meinel and Schnabel, 1998; Belej and Junger, 2006). Namely, the following motor tasks have been proposed for monitoring rhythmic ability:

12. Tapping hands to reproduce the movement rate of a targeted exercise
13. Tapping hands and feet to reproduce a given movement rate
14. Tapping hands to reproduce the rhythm of a specific, acyclic exercise
15. Running with a predetermined stride length marked by hoops (Figure 26)
16. Rope skipping to reproduce a given movement rate

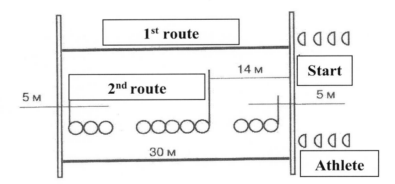

Figure 26. Running with a predetermined stride length (P. Hirtz, 1985)

1st attempt – running upon the 1st route; 2nd attempt – running upon the 2nd route, where the hoops predetermine the length of the strides. Comparison of running times equal to 1.2s indicate excellent rhythmic ability

Data of systematic studies confirm the high validity and reliability of the above tests and high trainability of the rhythmic coordination component (Belej and Junger, 2006). The typical coordination exercises presented below clearly reflect the methodological demands for training rhythmic ability in appropriate age groups.

8.2. Examples of exercises for 7-10 year old children

This offered selection of rhythmic exercises includes various combinations of rhythm reproduction in a standing position and while walking, running, or rope skipping (Table 25).

Table 25. Typical exercises for the development of rhythmic ability of 7-10 year old children

No	Exercise description	Comments
1	Rhythmic hand gripping of two arms while varying movement rate	Gripping tempo can be varied within one task and in separate attempts
2	Walking with arm rotations: one rotation for each step (a), two rotations for each step (b)	Reproduction of rhythm accuracy is controlled
3	Walking with arm/hand clapping: one clap for each step (a), one clap for two steps (b), one clap for three steps (c)	Reproduction of rhythm accuracy is controlled
4	In a standing position: left hand taps on the hip once, right hand taps on the hip twice	Reproduction of rhythm accuracy is controlled
5	In a standing position: left hand taps on the hip once, left leg taps on the floor once; right hand taps on the hip twice, right leg taps on the floor twice	Reproduction of rhythm accuracy is controlled
6	Walking with ball throwing. Athlete throws a ball upward for each step (a), every 2 steps (b), every 3 steps (c)	The throw's height is about 1m. The tempo increases from low to medium
7	The same drill while clapping the hands after each throw	The throw's height is about 1m. The tempo increases from low to medium
8	Throwing a ball at the wall from a distance of 3m a catching the ball after rebound	The rhythm of the throw/catch and reproduction accuracy are controlled
9	The same drill with a hand clap after each throw	The rhythm of the throw/catch and hand clap is controlled
10	Walking while changing the tempo: 4 steps – low tempo, 4 steps – medium, 4 steps - high	Low tempo – 90 step/min; medium tempo - 130 step/min; high tempo - 160 step/min
11	Running in place: 10s –low tempo, 10s – medium, 10s – high tempo	Low tempo – 100 step/min; medium tempo - 150 step/min; high tempo - 170 step/min
12	Running while changing speed: 10m –low speed, 10s – medium, 10s – high speed	Reproduction of rhythm accuracy is controlled
13	Rope skipping with acceleration (a), with deceleration (b), holding a constant tempo (c)	Reproduction of rhythm accuracy is controlled

Rhythmic hand gripping of both arms allows for the reproduction of various movement rates aiming to adapt children to pre-planned alterations, accelerations and decelerations (1st exercise). Similarly, walking with rhythmic arm rotations offers two different versions, such as one rotation for each step and two rotations for each step (2nd exercise). These rhythm variations are directed to enrich the coordination experience of children and enhance their ability to differentiate various movement patterns.

The 3rd exercise proposes the reproduction of various rhythmic patterns while walking and clapping the arms/hands. Each pattern presents an appropriate combination of steps and claps such as the execution of one clap during each step (a), one clap during each second step (b), and one clap during each third step (c). Acquisition of this motor skill leads to visible enhancement of rhythmic ability. Similarly, the 4th exercise proposes a rhythmic structure with separate actions of the two arms when the left hand taps on the hip once and the right hand taps on the hip twice. This drill can be done in a standing position or during slow walking.

The 5th exercise offers a pattern involving the rhythmic activity of the arms and legs. The athlete should be asked to perform a hand tap on the hip with the left arm and tap on the floor with the left leg. Then, the athlete should make two taps on the hip with the right hand followed by two taps on the floor with the right leg. Execution of all the above exercises should lead to clear comprehension that rhythmic activity comprises movements of the arms, legs, and the whole body in various combinations.

A number of exercises introduce rhythmic activity associated with ball throwing. Namely, the 6th exercise proposes walking with upward ball throwing and catching during each step (a), every two steps (b), and every three steps (c). This rhythm pattern is modified in next exercise, where the athletes are asked to perform a hand clap after each throw, and prior to catching the ball (7th exercise). These variations of movement patterns are directed to adapt children to different rhythmic structures and enlarge their motor experience.

The 8th exercise presupposes rhythmic throwing and catching of a ball after rebound from the wall. This motor task also demands reactive ability and agility. Nevertheless, after initial acquisition, children are able to perform repeated throws at a medium tempo. Afterwards, several rhythm variations can be performed. Further skill acquisition allows for modification of this drill including a hand clap after each throw before catching the ball (9th exercise).

Movement rate variations allow for diversification of the rhythmic preparation program. The 10th exercise demands changing the tempo (from low to medium and high) while walking. This exercise can be performed while walking in place and with forward displacement. In both cases, conscious control of tempo variation is required.

The next two exercises propose running while changing the tempo from low to medium to high. The 11th exercise suggests running in place, whereas the 12th exercise requires running with forward displacement. In both cases, changes in tempo should be performed every 10s; the total duration of running bouts is about 30s. The last (13th) exercise also adapts children to rhythm variations during rope skipping that should be done with acceleration (a), with deceleration (b), and holding a constant tempo (c). Each phase of performance should last about 20s.

8.3. Examples of exercises for 11-14 year old children

This age category is characterized by a relatively larger experience in various rhythmic activities. Correspondingly, the offered selection of exercises contains various rhythmic patterns of relatively higher complexity using available equipment and interaction with partners (Table 26).

Table 26. Typical exercises for development of rhythmic ability in 11-14 year old children

No	Exercise description	Comments
1	In standing position: 3 arm rotations forward and 3 arm rotations backward, changing the tempo	Drill's duration – 30s increasing the tempo from low to high
2	The same exercise with execution of a jump after every 3 rotations	Drill's duration – 30s increasing the tempo from low to high
3	Walking while raising a straight leg with execution of a hand clap under the leg	Tempo increases from low to medium, rhythm accuracy is controlled
4	Serial semi-squats raising a medicine ball up and lowering it down	Reproduction of rhythm accuracy is controlled
5	The same exercise with a medicine ball throw up and catching it while lowering the body	Throws' height is about 1m, reproduction of rhythm accuracy is controlled
6	Passing of the medicine ball to a partner with one arm and catching it with two arms, varying the tempo	The distance between partners is 6m. Shortening the distance between partners, increase the tempo
7	The same exercise with throwing and catching of two medicine balls	The distance between partners is 4-5m. Rhythm accuracy is controlled
8	Serial lifting of a barbell in a standing position up to shoulder height	Convenient rhythm of lifting should be maintained
9	Ball dribbling in a uniform tempo (a), increasing the tempo (b), decreasing the tempo (c)	The bout duration is 30s; the rhythm variations are controlled
10	Serial jumps on two legs changing the rhythm of performance	Rhythm variations: slow, faster, slow, faster
11	Serial jumps onto a gymnastics bench and back down, changing the rhythm of performance	Rhythm variations: slow, faster, slow, faster
12	Hanging on a high horizontal bar, execution of 10-12 body swings holding constant rhythm	The swings' amplitude and frequency should be medium
13	Execution of three body rolls holding a stable rhythm of performance	Reproduction of rhythm accuracy is controlled
14	Rope skipping with predetermined changes in the skips' frequency	Proposed skipping variation: slow-faster-faster-slower

The 1st exercise demands execution of arm rotations forward and backward while changing the tempo within one attempt and within separate trials. The athletes should receive experience in differentiation and variation of rhythm patterns. Inclusion of a jump performance every third arm rotation modifies the performance rhythm and increases its complexity (2nd exercise).

The 3rd exercise modifies usual walking by demanding raising a straight leg up every step and clapping the hands under the leg. This sophisticated rhythmic pattern demands accentuated proprioceptive and visual control. A number of repetitions lead to skill automatization when a rhythmic pattern of exercise can be easily modified.

The 4th exercise proposes execution of serial semi-squats while holding a medicine ball and raising it while lowering the body and lowering it during leg extension. This rhythmic pattern is modified in the 5th exercise, where an athlete throws a medicine ball upward and catches it during leg extension. In both, cases stability of the rhythmic pattern should be provided.

In the 6th exercise, an athlete should pass the medicine ball to a partner with one arm and catch the ball with two arms. The throws' tempo should gradually increase within each trial. This rhythmic pattern is modified in next exercise (7th) where the partners should throw and catch two medicine balls.

Repeated lifting of a barbell to shoulder height should be performed with a weight of about 30% of 1RM (8th exercise). The tempo and duration of this exercise should correspond to the age of the trainees and last about 30-40s. The athletes should be focused on rhythm stability and rational technical performance.

In the 9th exercise, the athletes should perform ball dribbling in three modifications: keeping a uniform tempo (a), increasing the tempo (b), decreasing the tempo (c). As a result, they should become acquainted with three variations of a rhythmic pattern.

The 10th exercise contains repeated two-legged jumps while changing the rhythm of performance. The initial 3-4 jumps should be done at a low tempo, then the frequency should increase to a medium tempo and the last 3-4 jumps should be performed at a high tempo. The whole rhythmic structure of this motor task reflects the increasing intensity of performance. A similar drill demands the execution of serial jumps to a gymnastics bench and back down, changing the rhythm of performance (11th exercise). The athletes should perform 3-4 jumps at a low tempo and 3-4 jumps at a higher tempo. This combination should be repeated 2-3 times. Both exercises adapt the athletes to conscious regulation of rhythmic activity during whole body performance.

The 12th exercise proposes execution of body swings while hanging on a high horizontal bar keeping a constant rhythm and stable amplitude of body displacement. Thus, the athletes should realize that the stability in the movements' reproduction largely contributes to the consistency of performance rhythm.

Maintenance of a stable performance rhythm is the primary goal of the 13th exercise, which demands the execution of three continuous body rolls. For several athletes, this task is associated with certain coordinative difficulty. Correspondingly, provision of rhythmic performance demands both mental concentration and increased proprioceptive control. Similarly, the next (14th) exercise demands predetermined changes of movement tempo during rope skipping. As a result of this coordination training, the athletes should enhance their ability of rhythm regulation.

8.4. Examples of exercises for 15-19 year old athletes

This category of athletes already has a relatively high level of rhythmic competence. Correspondingly, the offered selection of exercises requires larger mobilization of physical and mental recourses during appropriate coordination training (Table 27).

Table 27. Typical exercises for development of rhythmic ability of 15-19 year old athletes

No	Exercise description	Comments
1	Forward arm rotations combined with walking, increasing the movements' rate	Drill's duration – 30s increasing the tempo from low to high
2	Forward arm rotations combined with jumps on two legs increasing the movements' rate	Drill's duration – 30s increasing the tempo from low to high
3	Backward jumping on two legs with execution of a hand clap after each jump	Tempo increases from low to medium, rhythm accuracy is controlled
4	Walking on the hands when the legs are supported by a partner	Steps' tempo increases from low to medium
5	Throwing a medicine ball upward at a low (a), medium (b) and submaximal frequency (c)	Throws' height is about 1m, reproduction of rhythm accuracy is controlled
6	Running bouts of 20m, gradually increasing stride length	Lengthening the strides modifies the rhythm of running
7	Serial lifts of a barbell in a standing position to shoulder height	Lifts' tempo increases from low to medium
8	Hanging on a high horizontal bar, execution of 10-12 body swings holding a constant rhythm	The swings' amplitude should be near to maximal. Swings' rhythm should be constant within one attempt.
9	Passing of a medicine ball to a partner from a standing position (a), kneeling (b), and in a sitting position (c)	The throws' tempo varies from low to medium
10	Running 20m forward, backward, and sideways, changing the tempo	The tempo varies from low to high
11	Rope skipping, increasing the tempo on one leg (a), on two legs (b)	The tempo varies from low to high
12	Serial jumps onto a gymnastics bench and back down	The rhythm reproduction accuracy is controlled
13	Serial jumps over a gymnastics bench	The rhythm reproduction accuracy is controlled
14	Dribbling a ball at a constant tempo, increasing the tempo in subsequent attempts	The rhythm reproduction accuracy is controlled

The initial exercise presupposes forward arm rotations combined with walking while increasing the movements' rate from low to high. This gradual tempo variation produces enhancement of rhythm perception and increased proprioceptive control. Replacement of walking to two-legged jumping allows for a modification of this drill and its rhythmic structure (2nd exercise). The next exercise increases the complexity of the movement pattern offering execution of backward jumps on two legs with hand-clapping after each jump (3rd exercise).

The 4th exercise demands more pronounced physical efforts and interaction with a partner who should support the legs of the athlete while they walk on their hands, maintaining a constant movement rhythm.

The next motor task demands the execution of medicine ball throws upward at a varying movement rate. The athletes should increase the throwing tempo from low to medium and submaximal (5th exercise). Eventually, the increase in the throwing frequency will demand a reduction in the throwing height, which leads to an appropriate modification of the rhythmic pattern of the exercise.

Running while gradually increasing stride length presents one more approach to modification of the rhythmic structure of a motor task (6th exercise). Lengthening of the strides causes an increase in flight time and appropriate changes in movement rhythm, which should be marked by trainees.

Lifting a barbell is a widely used exercise for athletes of this age category. The 7th exercise proposes repeated lifts of a barbell in a standing position to shoulder height while maintaining a constant, convenient rhythm. The barbell weight should be about 30% of 1RM and the drill's duration, 20-30s.

The 8th exercise that should be performed while hanging on a high horizontal bar includes the execution of 10-12 body swings with an amplitude near to maximal. The athletes should select an appropriate movement rate and perform the exercise while holding a constant rhythm. The rhythm pattern can be modified in subsequent attempts, focusing on stable and technically correct performance.

The 9th exercise proposes passing of a medicine ball by two partners in three different conditions, i.e. in a standing position (a), kneeling (b), and seated (c). In all cases, the athletes should maintain a constant rhythm that should be the same, independently of external conditions of performance.

A combination of different running modes reinforces the ability to select appropriate rhythm patterns that are suitable for current conditions. The 10th exercise contains running bouts forward, backward, and sideways demanding a rational and stable rhythmic pattern in each performance. Similarly, the execution of rope skipping on one leg and on two legs while changing the skips' tempo requires adjustment to variable rhythm conditions within one performance and in subsequent attempts (11th exercise).

Serial jumps onto a gymnastics bench and back down as well as jumps over a gymnastics bench (12th and 13th exercises) presuppose acquisition of a rational rhythm pattern, although these drills require substantial physical efforts and spatial accuracy.

The 14th exercise includes dribbling a ball while maintaining a constant tempo within the trial and increasing the tempo in subsequent attempts. Accurate rhythm reproduction is highly demanded as a part of efficient coordination training.

Chapter 9 - Evaluation and development of agility

Agility is characterized as the ability to rapidly change movement direction and react to pre-planned or sudden stimuli. Its evaluation and development clearly reflect this methodological particularity.

9.1. Evaluation of agility

Typical motor tasks for evaluation of agility can be subdivided into two separate groups:

- Motor tasks demanding rapid change of movement direction;

- Motor tasks demanding connection of various movements as a rapid reaction to pre-planned or sudden stimuli.

The following motor tests are the most popular and widely used for the evaluation of various forms of agility in research and practice (Belej, Junger, 2006; Lyakh, 2006):

17. Three forward body rolls;
18. Rapid change in body position (RCBP), namely: from lying in a supine position, get up to a vertical standing position (1), lowering the body to a lying prone position (2), rise up to a vertical standing position (3), lowering the body to a lying supine position (4);
19. 3x10m Shuttle run.

The norms for identification of high-level performance in the above motor tests are presented below (Table 28).

Table 28. Estimates of high level agility based on several motor tests (seconds)
(Based on Belej and Junger, 2006; Lyakh, 2006)

Age	Gender	3 body rolls	RCBP	Shuttle run 3×10m
10	M	3.6	15.4	8.6
	F	4.1	18.7	9.1
14	M	3.4	14.7	7.7
	F	3.8	18.5	8.7
17	M	3.3	13.4	7.2
	F	3.6	18.0	8.4
20	M	3.2	13.0	7.0
	F	3.3	18.0	8.3

Correspondingly, the selection of exercises directed toward the development of agility in different age groups include various motor tasks that require rapid change of direction, rapid reaction to external stimuli, or both (Tables 27-29).

9.2. Examples of exercises for 7-10 year old children

The age range of 7-10 years is very favorable for the development of agility due to the high sensitivity of both girls and boys to these types of workloads. The offered selection of typical exercises is predisposed by the above-mentioned circumstances and the practical needs of various sports (Table 29).

Table 29. Typical exercises for development of agility of 7-10 year old children

No	Exercise description	Comments
1	Execution of 3 body rolls forward as fast as possible	Rolling accuracy and performance time is controlled
2	Execution of 3 body rolls backward as fast as possible	Rolling accuracy and performance time is controlled
3	Serial ball throws at a wall from a distance of 3m, catching rebound	The number of throws and performance time of 10 cycles is controlled
4	The same exercise with a hand clap after each throw	Performance time of 10 cycles is controlled
5	From lying in a supine position, moving to a standing position	Performance time of 10 cycles is controlled
6	From lying in a prone position, moving to a standing position	Performance time of 10 cycles is controlled
7	Throwing a ball upward, execution of a 180 degree body turn and catching the ball	Performance accuracy is controlled
8	Two partners stand back to back with one ball. Partners turn their upper bodies and pass the ball one to each other on both sides	The frequency of ball passing increases from medium to maximum
9	Standing high jump with execution of body rotation with maximal amplitude	The amplitude of body rotation is controlled
10	Serial two-legged jumps, clapping the hands behind the body prior to landing	Performance frequency increases from low to maximum
11	Running along a gymnastics bench on all fours	Performance speed increases from medium to maximum
12	Rolling a ball with the arms for a 10m distance, overcoming 4 obstacles	Performance time is controlled
13	Slalom running a 15m distance around 4 obstacles	Performance time and accuracy are controlled
14	Slalom dribbling a 15m distance around 4 obstacles (Figure 27)	Performance time and accuracy are controlled

The initial two exercises offer execution of body rolls forward and backward as fast as possible, aiming to manifest elementary agility in young athletes. Taking into account their restricted athletic experience, these motor tasks can provide relevant indications of coordination competence.

Serial ball throws at a wall when catching the rebound can be done standing in place or moving along the wall (3rd exercise). In both cases, the obtained throws' frequency provides an indicator of individual agility. Insertion of a hand clap after each throw allows for a modification of this exercise and an increase its complexity (4th exercise).

Exercises with rapid changes of body position, from a lying to standing position, are very typical for agility training (5th and 6th exercises). The initial tempo of body position change is usually low and increases to a medium level after a number of repetitions. Subsequent attempts can be performed with increased frequency. These exercises can be recommended for independent home preparation.

The 7th exercise demands high accuracy and rapidness in execution of an upward ball throw with a rapid, 180 degree body turn prior to catching the ball. Serial execution of this motor task leads to its automatization and increased stability of performance.

The 8th exercise requires rational interaction of two athletes. Standing back to back with one ball, they should turn their upper bodies and pass the ball one to another to both sides. Acquisition of this coordination skill demands mental and physical efforts and leads to agile and rapid performance.

A standing high jump with execution of body rotation with maximal amplitude requires a powerful take-off with rapid turning of the body prior the landing. This 9th exercise also serves as an indicator of agility in any age category.

The 10th exercise contains serial two-legged jumps while clapping the hands behind the body prior to landing. These linked activities of the arms and legs provide valuable stimulation of coordination ability. An increase in the movement rate leads to more agile and rapid performance.

Running along a gymnastics bench on all fours inserts fun/attraction to coordination training (11th exercise). Moreover, this comic locomotion allows for diversification of coordination training and provides valuable input to agility enhancement.

The 12th exercise includes rolling of a ball with the arms for a 10m distance while overcoming 4 obstacles in a slalom route. This original motor task provides much freedom in coordination of forward displacement, slalom-shape movement, and manipulations with the ball. Its inclusion into the coordination program is highly recommended.

The final two drills propose execution of slalom running (13th exercise) and slalom dribbling (14th exercise) over a 15m distance and around 4 obstacles. This change of direction movement pattern reflects the principal demand of agility training and provides a sufficiently high stimulatory effect for this group of athletes.

9.3. Examples of exercises for 11-14 year old children

The offered selection of agility exercises for older children reasonably includes motor tasks of higher complexity and higher intensity. It is worth noting that the metabolic component plays an important role in agility related motor tasks. Another factor, proprioceptive neuromuscular control, largely determines the manifestation of agility and its importance was taken into account in the selection of the exercises presented below (Table 30).

Table 30. Typical exercises for development of agility of 11-14 year old children

No	Exercise description	Comments
1	Execution of 3 body rolls forward and 3 body rolls backward in the same direction as fast as possible	Rolling accuracy and performance time is controlled
2	The same exercise with maximal body displacement	Rolling accuracy and total body displacement are controlled
3	Repeated ball throws at a wall from a 4m distance, catching rebound	Performance time of 12 cycles is controlled
4	Execution of the same exercise from a 3m distance and in a seated position	Performance time of 12 cycles is controlled
5	From lying in a supine position, moving to a standing position followed by moving to a prone position and again to a standing position	Performance time of 12 cycles is controlled
6	Four running steps, two body rolls and running along a gymnastics bench	Performance time and accuracy are controlled
7	Running forward and backward along a gymnastics bench that is inclined 30 degrees	Performance time is controlled
8	Running along a gymnastics bench that is inclined 30 degrees on all fours	Performance time is controlled
9	Dribbling a ball on a slalom route for 20m with 4 obstacles	Performance time is controlled
10	Dribbling a soccer ball on a slalom route for 20m with 4 obstacles (Figure 27)	Performance time is controlled
11	The same exercise with shooting at a goal from an 8m distance	Performance time and accuracy of shooting are controlled
12	Repeated two-leg jumps for 10m as fast as possible: forward (a), backward (b), sideways (c)	The number of jumps and performance time are controlled
13	Two partners standing face-to-face, raise one leg that is held by their partner; they perform semi squats (a), jumps (b) (Figure 28)	The movement rate increases gradually from low to medium following cues of the coach
14	Standing high jump with maximal range of body rotation	The amplitude of body rotation is controlled

The initial exercise calls for the execution of 3 body rolls forward and 3 body rolls backward in the same direction with maximal speed. Measuring performance time provides an objective indication of an agility-related factor and provides motivation for gradual enhancement in subsequent attempts. The 2nd exercise presupposes execution of the same exercise with maximal forward displacement following 6 body rolls. This additional demand causes deceleration of the movement; the athletes will be able compare the effects of the faster and the longer performances.

Repeated ball throws at a wall when catching the rebound is a typical, agility-demanding task (3rd exercise) where movement rate provides an objective indication of mastery. However, restriction of the area when the throw-catch actions are performed in a seated position (4th exercise) modifies the motor task, demanding higher accuracy and more pronounced proprioceptive and visual control.

The 5th exercise demands rapid changes of body positions from lying supine to standing followed by moving to lying prone and again to a standing position. This sequence of bodily changes should be performed using rational and rapid movements with indication of performance time. A similar motor task is offered in the 6th exercise, where the movement sequence includes four running steps, two body rolls and running along a gymnastics bench. Repeated execution of this drill leads to substantial shortening of performance time and, correspondingly, enhancement of agility.

Modification of external conditions evokes necessity in the acquisition of a new agility related motor skill. Namely, running forward and backward along a gymnastics bench that is inclined 30 degrees requires adequate adjustment of locomotor activity and mental concentration (7th exercise). Similarly, running along a gymnastics bench that is inclined 30 degrees on all fours adds novelty and attraction to the agility training program (8th exercise).

The next two exercises demand manifestation of agility in slalom-shape tasks. The athletes will dribble a ball on a slalom route (9th exercise) and/or dribble a soccer ball (10th exercise, Figure 27). In both cases, execution of a number of attempts leads to visible enhancement of movement technique and shortening of performance time.

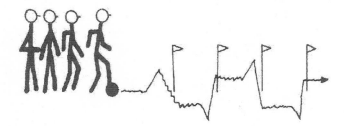

Figure 27. Dribbling a soccer ball on a slalom route for a 20m distance

The 11th exercise contains slalom-shape soccer dribbling with shooting at a goal from an 8m distance. This final component of the motor task inserts additional complexity and attraction to the practice routine.

Repeated two-leg jumps for 10m should be performed with forward, backward and sideways displacement (12th exercise). This combination of jumping performances can be done within one attempt or in series of separate, subsequent trials. In both cases, the jumping tempo should be controlled, aiming to gradually increase the jumping frequency and intensity of the motor performance.

The 13th exercise demands interaction of two partners who stand face-to-face on one leg while holding the second leg of their partner (Figure 28). Maintaining this position, the partners should perform semi squats (a) or jumps (b). In both cases, the athletes should provide rational interaction, increasing the movement rate from low to medium in semi squats and from medium to high in jump performance.

Figure 28. Execution of single-leg semi-squats and jumps with a partner

The last (14th) exercise in this set demands the execution of a standing high jump with maximal range of body rotation. This highly indicative motor task provides valuable information on individual agility combined with a pronounced explosive effort during take-off and is recommended for general monitoring of coordination competence.

9.4. Examples of exercises for 15-19 year old athletes

Athletes of this age category usually have extensive experience in coordination training. Apparently, this category of more matured athletes has completed many exercises for sport-specific agility. Nevertheless, enhancement of general agility using diversified training means remains important. Thus, the setting of more advanced agility-related motor tasks is presented below (Table 31).

Table 31. Typical exercises for development of agility of 15-19 year old athletes

No	Exercise description	Comments
1	Dribbling a ball on a slalom route for 20m with 4 obstacles, ending with shooting the ball to a basketball hoop from 3m away	Dribbling and shooting accuracy are controlled
2	Dribbling a soccer ball on a slalom route for 20m with 4 obstacles, ending with shooting the ball at a goal from 8m away	Dribbling and shooting accuracy are controlled
3	Serial ball throws at a wall from 4m away followed by a hand clap prior catching rebound	Performance time of 12 cycles is controlled
4	Execution of the same exercise from 3m away in a seated position	Performance time of 12 cycles is controlled
5	Jump over a bench with a ball throw up and catching it during the landing	Throw's, jump's and catching accuracy are controlled
6	Throw a ball upward/forward with execution of a body roll and catching the ball	Performance accuracy of whole combination is controlled
7	Dribbling of two balls with two arms in place	Task's duration is 30s
8	Dribbling of two balls with two arms for 20m	Performance time is controlled
9	Throwing and catching of two balls with a partner (Figure 13)	Distance between partners is about 7m. Tempo increases from low to medium
10	Rope skipping trying to complete the minimum amount of skips for 40s	A number of skips is controlled
11	Shuttle run 5x5 m and 5x10m	Performance time is controlled
12	Lying in supine position, throwing a medicine ball from the legs to arms and back	Performance time of 10 cycles is controlled
13	Juggling two balls, throwing them with two arms upward	Performance time of 10 cycles is controlled
14	Standing high jump with maximal range of body rotation	The amplitude of body rotation is controlled
15	The 1st partner sits on the 2nd one in "rider" position and performs dribbling (Figure 29)	This task is performed in place and moving forward and backward
16	Overcoming of an agility route with a number of artificial obstacles (Figure 30)	Execution accuracy and performance time should be controlled

The 1st exercise includes slalom-shape dribbling over a 20m route, ending with shooting the ball to a basketball hoop from 3m away. Accurate shot is required; an athlete can make two additional attempts until they have a successful performance. A similar motor task includes soccer dribbling with shooting at a goal from 8m away (2nd exercise). In both cases, inclusion of the ending shot increases the emotional circumstances of the performance, demanding higher accuracy and mental concentration.

The 3rd exercise includes execution of repeated ball throws at a wall followed by a hand-clap prior to catching the rebound. This agility demanding drill can be fulfilled by increasing the tempo from medium to high. The 4th exercise presupposes execution of the same task in a seated position. This modification of the external conditions reinforces the demands to proprioceptive control and throw-catch accuracy.

In the 5th exercise, the athletes should jump over a bench while throwing a ball up and catching it during the landing. This motor task demands high accuracy in ball throwing in addition to catching on the other side of the bench. The initial attempts should be performed at a relatively low tempo, which should be increased in subsequent trials. Measuring of movement rate variation provides a valuable indication of agility enhancement. Similarly, the 6th exercise demands precise throwing of a ball in an upward/forward direction that allows the athlete to catch the ball after rapid execution of a body roll. Both motor tasks require appropriate acquisition of new motor skills and stimulate agility-related progression.

The next two exercises include dribbling of two balls with two arms in place (7th exercise) or while moving forward (8th exercise). These motor tasks largely exploit visual and proprioceptive control and require high mental concentration. Correspondingly, at least the initial attempts should be fulfilled in well-rested conditions.

The 9th exercise includes throwing and catching of two balls with a partner (Figure 13). Acquisition of this unusual motor task requires appropriate cues and control from the coach during the initial attempts. Nevertheless, subsequent trials can be successfully fulfilled, gradually increasing the tempo and duration of performance.

Rope skipping is usually a very familiar exercise for this category of athletes. However, its execution at a reduced tempo requires appropriate adjustment of the movement pattern and is associated with distinct coordination complexity (10th exercise).

Shuttle runs of 5x5m and 5x10m are typical drills with rapid changes of direction that are popular in agility training (11th exercise). Measurement of performance time in these drills is highly recommended for monitoring and individual motivation of the athletes.

The next exercise demands creativity - throwing a medicine ball with the legs while lying in a supine position (12th exercise). The throw should be properly directed toward the arms; furthermore, the ball should be directed back to legs for a subsequent throw to arms. This original task usually raises vivid interest in athletes.

Juggling with two balls by throwing them upward and catching with two arms is an original motor task that demands accentuated motor control, mental concentration and manual dexterity (13th exercise). Acquisition of this skill requires a number of preliminary attempts; subsequent attempts can be fulfilled at a convenient tempo. Further training allows for an increase in movement rate and stability of performance.

A standing high jump with maximal range of body rotation has already been considered an indicative trial that can be recommended for agility monitoring in any age group (14th exercise).

The next exercise presupposes interaction of two partners, where the 1st partner sits on the 2nd partner in a "rider" position and performs dribbling (15th exercise, Figure 29). Further acquisition of this skill allows for organization of performance in the form of a competition between couples.

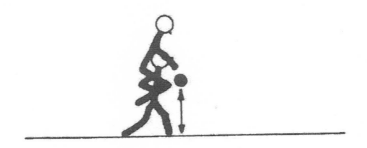

Figure 29. Execution of dribbling by a partner who sits in a "rider" position

The last (16th) exercise proposes execution of a complex, multilateral task including overcoming of a number of artificial obstacles (Figure 30). The coach should control the accuracy and duration of performance. This multilateral task can be reasonably used for monitoring of athletic agility.

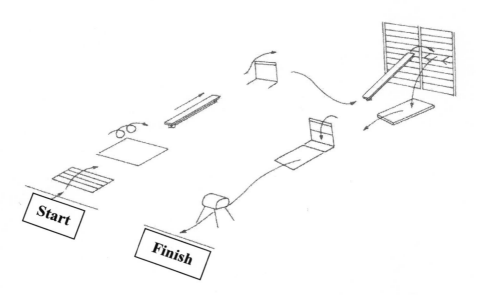

Figure 30. Agility route with overcoming of artificial obstacles
1st step – long jump over the "ditch"; 2nd step - forward body roll; 3rd step - running along gymnastics bench; 4th step – jump over the barrier; 5th step – running along inclined gymnastics bench; 6th step – drop jump on the targeted surface; 7th step – climb over the barrier; 8th – squeeze through gymnastics horse; 9th step – running to finish

Concluding this section, it is worth noting that agility training should be an indispensable part of athletic preparation in any sport. In this context, two relevant remarks should be made. On one hand, execution of very familiar exercises allows for maintenance of the available level of agility as a background for sport-specific, technical preparation. On the other hand, further enhancement of the coordination base requires involvement of new exercises that require appropriate efforts for acquisition and refinement.

Chapter 10 - Evaluation and development of complex motor reaction and voluntary muscle relaxation

Complex motor reaction is considered the ability to react accurately and rapidly to stimuli recognized from among other signals.

10.1. Evaluation of complex motor reaction

Complex motor reaction can be evaluated following analysis of an athlete's behavior in unpredictable competitive situations, particularly, in ball games and combat sports. More precise and objective evaluation can be fulfilled using sport-specific research designs and computerized testing procedures. One of the most widely used tools is the computerized Vienna test system (Schuhfriegd, 1996). The program demands recognition of the correct stimulus, from among others, and a rapid reaction to it. Another practical and acceptable approach is the relatively simple procedure of catching a falling ruler (Figure 31).

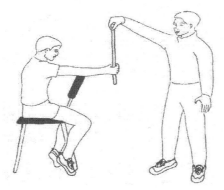

Figure 31. Catching a falling ruler

Simultaneously with command, the coach releases the ruler. The athlete should catch the ruler as fast as possible; the distance of the ruler's fall provides an indication of motor reaction.

In the second test, an athlete should catch a rolling ball that is placed on the upper point between two sloped gymnastic benches (Figure 32).

The estimates characterizing a high level of complex motor reaction measured by means of the motor tests described above are presented below (Table 32).

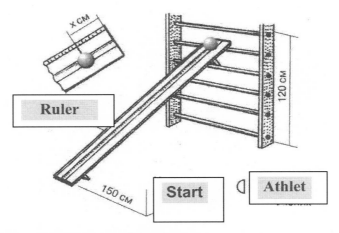

Figure 32. Catching the rolling ball (P.Hirtz, 1985)

An athlete stands facing away from the ball; simultaneously with command, the coach releases the ball and it starts to roll; the athlete should turn and catch ball as soon as possible. The distance the ball rolls provides an indication of motor reaction.

Table 32. Estimates of a high level of motor reactivity based on several motor tests
(based on Belej and Junger, 2006; Lyakh, 2006)

Age	Gender	Catching the falling ruler (cm)	Catching the rolling ball (cm)
10	M	16.4	120
	F	17.4	130
14	M	15.0	114
	F	15.5	120
17	M	14.2	110
	F	15.3	116
20	M	13.9	105
	F	13.2	111

Although human motor reactivity largely depends on heredity related factors, purposeful coordination training allows an athlete to substantially improve these functions (Table 6). The groups of appropriate exercises presented below substantially enrich the training repertoire of creative coaches and provide for more efficient athletic preparation.

10.2. Examples of exercises for 7-10 year old children

The offered selection of exercises proposes various motor tasks where children should adequately react to an external signal and/or an available training situation (Table 33).

Table 33. Typical exercises for development of complex motor reaction of 7-10 year old children

No	Exercise description	Comments
1	Execution of body roll; following one whistle – forward; following two whistles – backward	Speed and accuracy of reaction are controlled
2	Change direction of running; one whistle – turn left; two whistles – turn right	Speed and accuracy of reaction are controlled
3	The same exercise while dribbling	Speed and accuracy of reaction are controlled
4	Serial ball throws at a wall, catching rebound; following one whistle – with one arm; two whistles – with two arms	Throw distance is about 3m. Speed and accuracy of reaction are controlled
5	Jumps near a gymnastics bench: one whistle – jump on the bench; two whistles – jump over the bench; three whistles – jump over the bench with body turn	Speed and accuracy of performance and reaction are controlled
6	Serial jumps following command of coach: one whistle – on left leg; two whistles – on right leg; three whistles – on both legs	This drill can be done in place or moving forward
7	Rope skipping following the command of the coach: one whistle – in place; two whistles – with forward displacement; three whistles – with backward displacement	Speed and accuracy of reaction are controlled
8	Serial throws ball up: one whistle – hand clap prior to catching; two whistles – with jump during the catch	Speed and accuracy of reaction are controlled
9	Drop jumps: one whistle – with arm swing; two whistles – without swing; three whistles – with body rotation	Drop jumps from a height of 70cm; body rotation on 180 degrees
10	Throwing a stick upward: one whistle – catch stick with one arm; two whistles – with two arms	Throws' tempo varies from low to medium
11	Athletes kneel: one whistle – jump onto two legs; two whistles – jump onto one leg	Jumps tempo varies from low to medium

The 1st exercise demands a rapid choice reaction, performing a forward body roll following one whistle or backward body roll following two whistles. Execution of this drill by a number of athletes allows a coach to immediately recognize more successful performers and affects motivation in less successful athletes. A similar situation will occur during execution of the 2nd and 3rd exercises where athletes should change direction of running or dribbling and turn left or right following one or two whistles from the coach. It is known that several trainees will react, not to the acoustic signal, but to the action of more rapid group-mates. This delayed reaction can be easily recognized by the coach, who can address appropriate cues for the less successful trainees.

The 4th exercise demands execution of repeated ball throws at a wall catching the rebound with one or two arms following one or two whistles, respectively. The movement rate should gradually increase from relatively slow to medium following the cues of the coach.

The 5th exercise presupposes rapid reaction and precise performance: jump on the bench following one whistle, jump over the bench following two whistles, and jump over the bench with a 180 degree body turn after three whistles.

The 6th exercise requires a choice reaction during the execution of serial jumps. Following one whistle from the coach, the athletes should jump on their left leg; following two whistles – on the right leg; and following three whistles – on both legs. The jumps' frequency should vary from low to medium. A similar task can be done during rope skipping (7th exercise). Following one whistle, the athletes should skip in place; following two whistles – with forward displacement; and following three whistles – with backward displacement.

The 8th exercise demands throwing a ball upward with variations of catching. Following one whistle, a hand clap should be done prior to the catch; following two whistles, the catch should be done during a jump.

Drop jumps should be performed from a height of 70cm (9th exercise). Following one whistle, the jump should be done with arms' swing; following two whistles – without swing;

following three whistles - with body rotation to 180 degrees. The total number of performances varies between 5 and 7.

The 10th exercise proposes throwing a stick upward and varying the catch mode: one whistle – with one arm; two whistles – with two arms. Similarly, a choice reaction is required in the 11th exercise, where athletes should kneel and perform a jump onto two legs following one whistle and jump onto one leg following two whistles. This last exercise is associated with explosive efforts and can be repeated 5-7 times.

10.3. Examples of exercises for 11-14 year old children

The offered selection of exercises includes motor tasks of higher complexity; a portion of the drills require interaction with a partner (Table 34). Of course, current control of performance quality is highly recommended. New exercises demand relatively high mental concentration and should be learned in a well-rested condition. After familiarity and skill acquisition, these exercises can also be practiced at the end of a workout combined with a cool-down.

Table 34. Typical exercises for development of complex motor reaction of 11-14 year old children

No	Exercise description	Comments
1	Execution of body rolls; one whistle – one roll, two whistles – two rolls, three whistles – three rolls	Speed and accuracy of reaction and performance are controlled
2	Actions during running; one whistle – semi squat; two whistles – full squat; three whistles – jump with 180 degree body rotation	Speed and accuracy of reaction and performance are controlled
3	Actions during dribbling: one whistle – throw ball upward, two whistles – throw ball upward with jump	Speed and accuracy of reaction and performance are controlled
4	Repeated ball throws at a wall, moving along the wall with sidesteps, catching rebound from wall	Throw distance is about 3m. Speed and accuracy of reaction are controlled
5	Two athletes stand face-to-face. Following the coach's signal, they throw balls upward, change position and catch the partner's ball	Distance between partners is about 1.5m
6	Rope skipping: one whistle – with forward displacement; two whistles – with backward displacement; three whistles – in place	Speed and accuracy of reaction and performance are controlled
7	Running starts from different positions: sitting on the floor, kneeling, lying in supine position	Speed and accuracy of reaction are controlled
8	Standing with back to the wall at a 3m distance; throw ball backward, turn the body and catch rebound	Throws tempo increases from low to medium
9	1st partner throws ball to wall; 2nd one catches rebound and passes ball to partner (Figure 17a)	Throws tempo increases from low to medium
10	Throwing of a tennis ball to rolling a medicine ball from a 3m distance	Partner pushes medicine ball that rolls slowly
11	Jumps along a circle-shaped route; two partners hold each other's shoulders: one whistle – jumps on left leg; two whistles – jumps on right leg; three whistles – jumps on two legs	The partners jump simultaneously in medium tempo.
12	Two athletes stand back-to-back 2m apart. 1st one throws ball up and backward; 2nd one turns and catches the ball	Throw's height is about 2m. Throw-catch frequency varies from low to medium

The 1st exercise demands execution of one body roll following one whistle, two rolls following two whistles, and three rolls after three whistles. The total number of rolls performed should be about 10-11. The 2nd exercise presupposes breaking during running and execution of appropriate actions such as a semi squat, a full squat and a jump with body rotation to 180 degrees following one, two, and three whistles, respectively. A similar task can be performed while dribbling (3rd exercise). Evidentially, manipulations with a ball increase the complexity of this drill.

The 4th exercise contains repeated ball throws at a wall, moving along the wall with sidesteps and catching the rebound from the wall. A throw distance of about 3m provides favourable conditions for motor reaction during the catch. Correspondingly, movement rate and drill intensity can be increased from medium to high.

The 5th exercise demands interaction of two partners who stand face-to-face. Following the signal of their coach, they should throw two balls upward, change their positions and catch their partner's ball. This task demands a pre-programmed reaction to the descending ball and their partner's movement.

Rapid recognition of acoustic signals during rope skipping is required in the 6th exercise, where the athletes should move forward following one whistle; move backward following two whistles, and skip in place after three whistles.

The 7th exercise is directed to enhance motor reaction when the athlete starts running from different positions, i.e. sitting on the floor, kneeling or lying in a supine position. This action demands the highly coordinated motor reaction of large muscle groups and provides a positive effect that can be utilized in different sports.

The next exercise demands throwing a ball backward to a wall from a 3m distance (8th exercise). The athlete should rapidly turn their body and catch the ball's rebound from the wall. This motor task of relatively high complexity usually requires a number of preliminary attempts for skill acquisition; subsequent attempts provide a high neuromuscular and emotional impact. A similar motor task can be done with a partner who throws a ball at the wall; the 2nd partner should catch the rebound and pass the ball to the 1st partner (9th exercise, Figure 17a).

The 10th exercise demands precise reaction to a moving object. An athlete should throw a tennis ball at a rolling medicine ball from a distance of 3m. Although the big ball should roll slowly, successful performance requires anticipation and high accuracy. This task can also serve as a test of motor reactivity for youth athletes.

The 11th exercise presupposes interaction of two partners who perform jumps along a circle-shape route while holding each other's shoulders. Following one whistle, they should jump on their left leg; following two whistles – jump on the right leg; and following three whistles they should jump on both legs.

In the last (12th) exercise, two athletes should stand back-to-back 2m apart. The 1st partner should throw a ball up and backward, whereas the 2nd partner should rapidly turn and catch the descending ball. This unusual motor task demands high reactivity combined with agility.

10.4. Examples of exercises for 15-19 year old athletes

The complex motor reaction of 15-19 year old athletes approaches the level of adult athletes; this was taken into account in the compilation of this selection of offered exercises for purposeful coordination training (Table 35).

Table 35. Typical exercises for development of complex motor reaction of 15-19 aged athletes

No	Exercise description	Comments
1	Execution of two body rolls and catching a ball passed by a partner	Speed and accuracy of reaction and performance are controlled
2	Actions during running: one whistle – running backward; two whistles – two jumps; three whistles – 360 degree body rotation	Speed and accuracy of reaction and performance are controlled
3	Actions during dribbling: one whistle – throw ball upward, two whistles – throw ball upward with 360 degree body rotation	Speed and accuracy of reaction and performance are controlled
4	Passing of two balls. Athlete A rolls ball to partner with foot; athlete B throws ball to partner who catches it and throws it back (Figure 33)	Distance between partners is about 5m. Partners pass balls with feet and arms simultaneously
5	Two athletes stand face-to-face. Following the signal of the coach, they throw balls upward, change position and catch their partner's ball	Distance between partners is about 3m
6	Running starts following the command of the coach from different positions: sitting on the floor, lying supine, lying prone	Speed and accuracy of reaction are controlled
7	3-4 athletes stand on a line. Coach throws ball upward and calls the name of the athlete who should catch the ball	Throw's height is about 3m. Catching accuracy is controlled
8	The same exercise but catching the ball should be done after its rebound from floor	Throw's height is about 2m. Catching accuracy is controlled
9	Athletes stand near a gymnastics bench; one whistle – jump on the bench, two whistles – jump over the bench	Jumps tempo increases from medium to high
10	Two athletes stand on a line. Coach throws ball upward; the athletes try to catch the ball as high as possible	Throw's height is about 3m. Distance between athletes is about 2m
11	Throwing a tennis ball at a rolling medicine ball from 3m away	Partner pushes medicine ball, which should roll with medium speed
12	2 partners stand face-to-face performing dribbling with one hand. After the signal of the coach, the 1st partner throws a 2nd ball to their partner who should catch it and throw back (Figure 34)	The distance between partners is about 5m. The athletes should react on the throw, continuing to dribble their own ball

The 1st exercise presupposes execution of two body rolls ending with catching a ball that is passed by a partner. The irritation of vestibular receptors produces a negative background for ball catching; this exercise should enhance the resistance of the motor reaction to vestibular aggravation.

The next two exercises demand manifestation of high motor reactivity while running (2nd exercise) or dribbling (3rd exercise). In the former, the athletes should run backward following one whistle, perform two jumps following two whistles, and a 360 degree body rotation after three whistles. During the dribbling exercise, the athletes are required to a throw ball upward after one whistle and throw a ball upward with a 360 degree body rotation following two whistles.

The 4th exercise includes passing two balls by two athletes where partner A rolls the ball by foot and partner B throws the ball with their hands. Thus, the partners continue to pass the balls by feet and by hands, enhancing their complex motor reaction (Figure 33).

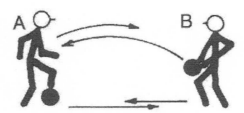

Figure 33. Passing of two balls by foot and by hand.

In the 5th exercise, two athletes standing face-to-face, throw two balls upward, change position and catch their partner's ball. This exercise was already offered for 11-14 year old athletes. However, the complexity of this motor task is increased for more mature performers by lengthening the distance between them from 1.5 to 3m.

The 6th exercise proposes execution of running starts from different positions such as sitting on the floor, lying supine, and lying prone. This motor task is associated with accentuated demands to the movement component of complex motor reaction.

In the next (7th) exercise, a number of athletes take part who stand on a line and wait for the command of a coach who throws a ball upward and calls out the name of an athlete. The athlete who is called should move forward and catch the ball. The same exercise is offered with modified demand; the catch should be made after the ball rebounds off the floor (8th exercise).

In the 9th exercise, athletes should stand near a gymnastics bench. Following one whistle, they should jump on the bench, following two whistles – jump over the bench. The tempo of performance gradually increases from medium to high.

The 10th exercise offers competition between two athletes who stand on a line. The coach throws a ball upward and the athletes jump up and forward, trying to catch the ball as high as possible. The 11th exercise was already offered for 11-14 year old athletes. It proposes throwing a tennis ball at a rolling medicine ball from 3m away. It can be suggested that throwing accuracy of more mature athletes should be higher than their younger counterparts.

In the last (12th) exercise, 2 partners, standing face-to-face, should dribble a ball with one hand. Following the signal of their coach, the 1st partner throws a 2nd ball to their partner, who should catch it and throw back (Figure 34). This exercise of increased complexity demands high accuracy in throwing, stable performance of dribbling, and high reactivity for ball catching. This task can be performed at a low to medium tempo.

Concluding this section, it is worth noting that exercises for motor reactivity form an important part of general coordination training in various sports. Depending on the goal of the coach, these exercises can be included in the warm-up, the main portion of the workout, or in the cool down. In any case, coaching creativity is the most important factor that determines the training compilation and its effect.

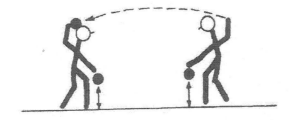

Figure 34. Execution of ball throwing combined with dribbling

10.5. Exercises for voluntary relaxation of muscles

In addition to the above-considered, basic CA, several training experts have also noted the ability of voluntary relaxation of muscles (Meinel and Schnabel, 1998; Lyakh, 2006). The Autors reasonably noted that voluntary relaxation of muscles largely affects the manifestation of both basic and sport-specific CA and can be improved following purposeful training. Although a review of the available literature provides limited information related to the repertoire of goal-oriented exercises, a selection of purposeful motor tasks can be offered based on the practical experiences of advanced coaches from various sports (Table 36).

Table 36. Typical exercises for voluntary relaxation of muscles

No	Exercise description	Comments
1	Shaking of body limbs, varying its frequency and amplitude	Can be performed in a standing, sitting, or lying position
2	Rapid transition from contraction to full relaxation of large muscle groups	This task is practiced separately for arms and legs
3	The same exercise combined with full expiration	Premature deep breath should be taken
4	High amplitude swings or rotations of relaxed arms	Can be performed in a standing position
5	High amplitude swings of relaxed leg	Can be performed standing on one leg with upper body support
6	Simultaneous contraction of a certain muscle group and full relaxation of another one	Both contraction and relaxation are voluntarily controlled
7	Relaxed jogging with short, frequent steps and shaking of arms	The neck muscles should be relaxed as well
8	1st partner is in a lying position; the 2nd one shakes his/her relaxed arm or leg	Shaking should be done varying its frequency and amplitude

The 1st exercise introduces one of the most popular motor tasks, offering shaking of body limbs such as arms or legs, varying its frequency and amplitude. This drill can be done in a standing, sitting, or even a lying position when the athlete shakes a body limb following the cues of the coach and individual experience.

The 2nd exercise presupposes a rapid transition from contraction of a muscle group to its voluntary relaxation, sequencing this task a number of times. This exercise can be combined with full expiration, which reinforces the effect of voluntary relaxation (3rd exercise).

The next two exercises involve high amplitude swings or rotations of relaxed arms (4th exercise) and high amplitude swings of a relaxed leg while standing on the other leg (5th exercise). In both cases, swings utilize the inertia of the moving limb.

The 6th exercise demands simultaneous contraction of a certain muscle group and full relaxation of another one. This combination of contraction and relaxation should enrich the individual's experience of neuromuscular regulation. The 7th exercise offers relaxed jogging with short, frequent steps combined with arm shaking. This drill actually produces relaxation of both the upper and lower body muscles.

Active muscle relaxation based on a partners' interaction has high practical importance. In the 8th exercise, one partner is in a lying position whereas the 2nd one shakes his/her relaxed arms or legs, varying the frequency and amplitude of shaking. Both supine and prone lying positions provide appropriate possibilities for shaking manipulations.

Summary

The available materials introduce descriptions and considerations of practical tools for monitoring and purposeful development of basic CA and voluntary muscle relaxation. Chapters 5-10 comprise guidelines for evaluation and training construction related to kinaesthetic differentiation, spatial orientation, body balance, rhythmic ability, agility and complex motor reaction. In all cases, appropriately selected motor tests and groups of purposeful exercises are offered for the age categories of 7-10, 11-14 and 15-19 years. Namely, the assessment of kinaesthetic differentiation presupposes measurement of accuracy of angular, linear, temporal and force characteristics during preprogrammed performance of various movements and efforts. A number of motor tests were proposed and verified with the aim to evaluate performance dexterity and accuracy. Similarly, evaluation of spatial orientation can be successfully fulfilled using specialized tests such as backwards throws of a tennis ball to a target without vision, rolling of three balls using both hands and feet along a slalom route, a shuttle run to arbitrarily called numbered balls, etc. In addition, a specialized computerized test has been proposed and verified for evaluating the ability of spatial orientation.

Evaluation and development of balance ability is an indispensable part of coordination training. A number of motor tests were proposed and implemented such as the following: Maintenance of static balance in a single-leg stance with eyes closed (Romberg test), maintenance of static balance in a bipedal stance on a balance board, walking forward and backward on the beam of upturned gymnastics benches, and execution of four full body turns on the beam of an upturned gymnastics bench. Table 21 presents estimates of high-level balance ability based on the above listed motor tests.

Rhythmic ability, as a true component of coordination competence, is responsible for the adjustment and reproduction of the temporal rhythm and movement rate of performance. Its evaluation has been fulfilled using the following motor tests: tapping hands to reproduce the movement rate of a targeted exercise, tapping hands and feet to reproduce a given movement rate, tapping hands to reproduce the rhythm of a specific acyclic exercise, running with a predetermined stride length marked by hoops, and rope skipping to reproduce a given movement rate.

Agility, which is characterized as the ability to rapidly change movement direction and react to pre-planned or sudden stimuli, can be evaluated using various sport-specific tests. The most popular, generalized tests include execution of three body rolls, rapid repeated changes of body positions from supine and prone lying positions to a vertical stand, and shuttle runs of 3×10m. Table 28 presents estimates of high level agility based on execution of the above mentioned motor tasks.

Complex motor reaction, the ability to react accurately and rapidly to stimuli that must be recognized from among other signals, can be evaluated using various computerized testing procedures and, particularly, the widely used Vienna test system. Other practical and acceptable motor tests offer relatively simple procedures such as catching a falling ruler or catching a rolling ball. Table 32 contains estimates characterizing a high level of motor reactivity based on utilization of the two above-mentioned tests.

The ability of voluntary relaxation of muscles is widely considered an additional factor that largely contributes to coordination competence of athletes. Table 36 offers a selection of goal-oriented exercises that allow an athlete to enhance this ability as well as facilitate the restoration processes following strenuous training workloads.

References

Abernethy B, Wood JM, Parks S. (1999). Can the anticipatory skills of experts be learned by novices? *Res Q Exerc Sport* ; 70(3):313-8.

Afonso J, Garganta J, Mesquita I. (2012). Decision-making in sports: the role of attention, anticipation and memory. *Bras J Kinanthropometry Hum Perform*; 14(5):592-601.

Agdiniotis I, Pollatou E, Gerodimos V, et al. (2009). Relationship between rhythmic ability and type of motor activities in preschool children. *Eur Psychomotricity J*; 2(1):24-34.

Arnold BL, Schmitz RJ. (1998). Examination of balance measures produced by the biodex stability system. *J Athl Training*; 33(4):323-7.

Bańkosz Z. (2012). The kinesthetic differentiation ability of table tennis players. *Hum Mov Quarterly*; 13(1):16-21

Belej M, Junger J. (2006). Motor tests of coordination abilities. Prešov: University in Prešov. Faculty of Sports.

Bernstein NA. (1947). On the construction of movements. Moscow: Medgiz.

Bernstein NA. (1967). The co-ordination and regulation of movements. Oxford: Pergamon Press.

Bernstein NA. (1991). On dexterity and its development. Moscow: FiS Publisher.

Blumenstein B, Orbach I. (2012). Mental practice in sport. Twenty case studies. New York: Nova Science Publishers Inc.

Broďáni J, Šimonek J. (2012). Prediction of coordination performance in ice-hockey players based on the structure of coordination capacities. Palestrica of the third millennium – Civilization and Sport; 13(4), 316-320

Buss DM, Shackelford TK. (1997). Human aggression in evolutionary psychological perspective. *Clin Psychol Rev*; 17(6):605-19.

Chałupka A, Różańska D, Rostkowska E. (2007). The rhythm of movement during aqua-aerobic classes. *Acta Univ Palacki Olomuc Gymn*; 37(3):27-36.

Chaouachi A, Brughelli M, Chamari K, Levin GT, et al. (2009). Lower limb maximal dynamic strength and agility determinants in elite basketball players. *J Strength Cond Res*; 23(5):1570-7.

Chkhaidze L. (1968). Coordination of voluntary movements in space flight conditions. Moscow: Nauka.

Durand-Bush N. (2000). The development and maintenance of expert athletic performance: Perceptions of Olympic and World champions, their parents and coaches. *Thesis of PhD dissertation*, Ontario: University of Ottawa.

Fourkas AD, Bonavolontà V, Avenanti A, et al. (2008). Kinaesthetic imagery and tool-specific modulation of corticospinal representations in expert tennis players. *Cereb Cortex*; 18(10):2382-90.

Frýbort P, Kokštejn J, Musálek M, et al. (2016). Does physical loading affect the speed and accuracy of tactical decision-making in elite junior soccer players? *J Sports Sci Med*; 15(2):320-26.

Gabbett T, Benton D. (2009). Reactive agility of rugby league players. *J Sci Med Sport*; 12(1):212-4.

Ghuntla TP, Mehta HB, Gokhale PA, et al. (2014). Influence of practice on visual reaction time. *J Mahatma Gandhi Inst Med Sci*; 19:119-22.

Gierzuk D.(2004). Coordination training as a factor streamlining of the goal-oriented and special stage during the shooting of wrestlers. *Thesis of PhD dissertation*. AWF, Krakow.

Gierczuk D, Bujak Z. (2013). The analysis of coordination training means used in the training of wrestlers. *J Combat Sports Martial Arts*; 4(1):19-23.

Gold JI, Shadlen MN. (2007). The neural basis of decision making. Annual Rev Neurosci; 30: 535-74.

Granacher U, Gollhofer A. (2011). Is there an association between variables of postural control and strength in adolescents? *J Strength Cond Res*; 25(6):1718-25.

Guellich A. (2013). Considering long-term sustainability in talent promotion. Implications for talent development in rowing. *Proceedings 18th FISA Youth Coaches Conference*; 2-24.

Guizani S, Bouzaouach I, Tenenbaum G, et al. (2006). Simple and choice reaction times under varying levels of physical load in high skilled fencers. *J Sports Med Phys Fitness*; 46(2):344-51.

Guskiewicz KM, Perrin DH. (1996). Research and clinical applications of assessing balance. *J Sport Rehab*; 5(1):45-63.

Haines C. (2003). Sequencing, co-ordination and rhythm ability in young children. *Child Care Health Dev*; 29(5):395-409.

Hijazi MM. (2013). Attention, Visual perception and their relationship to sport performance in fencing. *J Hum Kinet*; 39:195-201.

Hill-Haas SV, Dawson B, Impellizzeri FM, et al. (2011). Physiology of small-sided games training in football: a systematic review. *Sports Med*; 41(3):199-220.

Hirtz P. (1985). Koordinative Fähigkeiten im Schulsport: vielseitig, variationsreich, ungewohnt. Berlin: Volk und Wissen.

Hirtz P, Starosta W. (2002). Sensitive and critical periods of motor coordination development and its relation to motor learning. *J Hum Kinet*; 7:19-28.

Hollmann W, Hettinger T. (1990). Sportmedizin – Arbeits und Trainingsgrundlagen. (3rd ed). Stuttgart, New York: Schattauer.

Hrysomallis C. (2011). Balance ability and athletic performance. Sports Med; 41(3):221-32.

Issurin V. (2017). Athletic talent. Identification and its development. Michigan: Ultimate Athletes Concepts.

Ivry RB, Schlerf JE. (2008). Dedicated and intrinsic models of time perception. *Trends Cogn Sci*; 12(7):273-80.

Jansen P, Lehmann J. (2013). Mental rotation performance in soccer players and gymnasts in an object-based mental rotation task. *Adv Cogn Psychol*; 9(2):92-8.

Jones CM, Braithwaite VA, Healy SD. (2003). The evolution of sex differences in spatial ability. *Behav Neurosci*; 117(3):403-11.

Kida N, Oda S, Matsumura M. (2005). Intensive baseball practice improves the Go/Nogo reaction time, but not the simple reaction time. Brain Res Cogn Brain Res; 22(2):257-64.

Kleim JA, Barbay S, Cooper NR, et al. (2002). Motor learning-dependent synaptogenesis is localized to functionally reorganized motor cortex. *Neurobiol Learn Mem*; 77(1):63-77.

Kovacs EJ, Birmingham TB, Forwell L, et al. (2004). Effect of training on postural control in figure skaters: a randomized controlled trial of neuromuscular versus basic off-ice training programs. *Clin J Sport Med*; 14(4):215-24.

Kurtzer I, Herter TM, Scott SH. (2005). Random change in cortical load representation suggests distinct control of posture and movement. *Nat Neurosci*; 8(4):498-504.

Lech G, Jaworski J, Lyakh V, et al. (2011). Effect of the level of coordinated motor abilities on performance in junior judokas. *J Hum Kinet*; 30:153-160.

Lemmink KA, Visscher C. (2005). Effect of intermittent exercise on multiple-choice reaction times of soccer players. *Percept Mot Skills*; 100(1):85-95.

Lennemann LM, Sidrow KM, Johnson EM, et al. (2013). The influence of agility training on physiological and cognitive performance. *J Strength Cond Res*; 27(12):3300-9.

Linn MC, Petersen AC. (1985). Emergence and characterization of sex differences in spatial ability: a meta-analysis. *Child Dev*; 56(6):1479-98.

Ljakh W, Sadowski, E. (2000). About conceptions, problems, position and main principles of coordination training in sport. *Teoria I practica kultury fizicznei*; 5, 40-46.

Liach W. (2002). The effect of genetic and environmental factors on the development of motor coordination abilities in children aged 7-10 years. *Phys Education Sport*; 2: 265-267.

Ljach W, Witkowski Z. (2010). Development and training of coordination skills in 11- to 19-year-old soccer players. *Hum Physiol*; 36(1):64-71.

Lombardo M, Deaner R. (2014). You can't teach speed: sprinters falsify the deliberate practice model of expertise. *Peer J*; e445: 1-31.

Lord TR, Garrison J. (1998). Comparing spatial abilities of collegiate athletes in different sports. *Percept Mot Skills*; 86(3 Pt 1):1016-8.

Lyakh V. (2006). Coordination abilities: evaluation and development. Moscow: Division Publisher.

Lyach V. (2009).The concepts and effectiveness of coordination training in sport. In: Starosta W, Branislav J, editors. A new ideas in fundamentals of human movement and sport science: current issues and perspectives Belgrade: *Intern Assoc Sport Kinetics*; 184-188.

Lyakh V, Jaworski J, Wieczorek T.(2007). Genetic endowment of coordination motor abilities: a review of family and twin research. *J Hum Kinet;* 17: 25-40.

Matthews MJ, Matthews H, Yusuf M, et al. (2016). Traditional martial arts training enhances balance and neuromuscular control in female modern martial artists. *J Yoga Phys Ther*; 6(1):228.

Meinel K, Schnabel G. (1998). Bewegungslehre - Sportmotorik: Abriss einer theorie der sportlichen motorik unter pädagogischem aspekt. Berlin: Sportverlag.

Mekota K.(2000). Definitions and structure of motor dexterity. *Čes kinantropol*; 4(1):59-69.

Mekota K, Novosad J. (2005). Motoricke schopnosti. Olomouc: Univerzita Palackeho, Fakulta telesne kultury.

Mikolajec K., Ljach W. (1998). The influence of exercises with high coordinational complexity of the level of technical skills, game effectiveness and increase of motor abilities. In: J. Sadowski, W. Starosta, editors. Movement coordination in team Sport Games and Martial arts. Biała Podlaska, **Intern Assoc Sport Kinetics; 105-112.**

Moesch K, Elbe AM, Hauge MLT, et al. (2011). Late specialization: the key to success in centimeters, grams, or seconds (cgs) sports. *Scand J Med Sci Sports*; 21(6):E282–90.

Monteiro L, Chambel L, Cardoso M. (2011). Elite and sub-elite judokas: the factors behind international success. In: *Proceedings of 2011 Scientific Congress on martial arts and combat sports*. Viseu;.73-76.

Moreau D, Clerc J, Mansy-Dannay A, et al. (2012). Enhancing spatial ability through sport practice: Evidence for an effect of motor training on mental rotation performance. *J Ind Differences;* 33(2):83-8.

Mori S, Ohtani Y, Imanaka K. (2002). Reaction times and anticipatory skills of karate athletes. *Hum Mov Sci*; 21(2):213-30.

Muehlbauer T, Gollhofer A, Granacher U. (2013). Association of balance, strength and power measures in young adults. *J Strength Cond Res*; 27(3):582-9.

Mustafa K, Furmanek MP, Knapik A, et al. (2015). The Impact of the Swedish nassage on the kinaesthetic differentiation in healthy individuals. *Int J Ther Massage Bodywork*; 8(1): 2-11.

Nakamoto H, Mori S. (2008). Sport-specific decision-making in a Go/NoGo reaction task: difference among nonathletes and baseball and basketball players. *Percept Mot Skills*; 106(1):163-70.

Notarnicola A, Maccagnano G, Pesce V, et al. (2014). Visual- spatial capacity: gender and sport differences in young volleyball and tennis athletes and non-athletes. *BMC Res Notes*; 7:57.

Oliver JL, Meyers RW. (2009). Reliability and generality of measures of acceleration, planned agility, and reactive agility. *Int J Sports Physiol Perform*; 4(3):345-54.

Oreb G, Vlašić J, Cigrovski V, et al. (2011). Relationship between rhythm and learning alpine skiing technique. *6th FIEP Europ Congress*; 640-46.

Owen AL, Wong DP, Paul D, et al. (2014). Physical and technical comparisons between various-sided games within professional soccer. *Int J Sports Med*; 35(4):286-92.

Paillard T, Costes-Salon C, Lafont C, et al. (2002). Are there differences in postural regulation according to the level of competition in judoists? *Br J Sports Med*; 36(4):304-5.

Paillard T, Noé F, Rivière T, et al. (2006). Postural performance and strategy in the unipedal stance of soccer players at different levels of competition. *J Athl Training*; 41(2):172-76.

Pakosz P. (2013). EMG parameters and kinaesthetic differentiation during the free-throw of basketball players with various levels of athletic experience. *Cent Eur J Sport Sci Med*; 2(2):31-8.

Paul DJ, Gabbett TJ, Nassis GP. (2016). Agility in team sports: testing, training and factors affecting performance. *Sports Med*; 46(3):421-42.

Proske U. (2006). Kinaesthesia: the role of muscle receptors. Muscle Nerve; 34(5):545-58.

Proske U, Gandevia SC. (2009). The kinaesthetic senses. *J Physiol*; 587(Pt 17):4139-146.

Rana MS, Rajpoot YS. (2015). Impact and role of selected coordinative abilities in racket sports. *Intern J Sci Res*; 4(3):1466-69.

Rejman M, Klarowacz A, Zatoń K. (2012). An evaluation of kinaesthetic differentiation ability in monofin swimmers. *Hum Mov Quarterly*; 13(1):8-15.

Riewald S, Snyder C. (2014). The path to excellence: a view on the athletic development of U.S. Olympians who competed from 2000-2012. Initial report: results of the talent identification and development. *United States Olympic Committee.*

Savelsbergh GJ, Van Der Kamp J, Williams AM, et al. (2005). Anticipation and visual search behavior in expert soccer goalkeepers. *Ergonomics*; 48:1686-97.

Schnabel G. (2001). Motor coordination - The fundamental process of motor activity. In: Motor coordination in sport and exercise: Bologna: FIDAL; 89-106.

Schuhfriegd G. (1996). Manuals of the VIENNA Test Instrument Systems-DT. Modling, Austria: Schuhfried Eigenverlag.

Sheppard JM, Young WB. (2016). Agility literature review: classifications, training and testing. *J Sports Sci*; 24(9):919-32.

Sherry DF, Hampson E. (1997). Evolution and the hormonal control of sexually-dimorphic spatial abilities in humans. *Trends Cogn Sci*; 1(2):50-6.

Shrager Y, Bayley PJ, Bontempi B, et al. (2007). Spatial memory and the human hippocampus. *Proc Natl Acad Sci USA*; 104(8):2961-6.

Serpell BG, Young WB, Ford M. (2011). Are the perceptual and decision-making components of agility trainable? A preliminary investigation. *J Strength Cond Res*; 25(5):1240-8.

Silverman II, Choi J, Mackewn A, et al. (2000). Evolved mechanisms underlying wayfinding. further studies on the hunter-gatherer theory of spatial sex differences. *Evol Hum Behav*; 21(3):201-13.

Šimonek J. (2014). Coordination abilities in volleyball. Warsaw-Berlin: Walter de Gruyter & Co.

Söğüt M, Kirazci S, Korkusuz F. (2012). The Effects of rhythm training on tennis performance. *J Hum Kinet*; 33:123-32.

Söğüt M, Kirazci S. (2014). Sport participation and gender differences in rhythmic ability. *Hacettepe J Sport Sciences*; 25(1):36-42.

Sommer M, Häger C, Rönnqvist L. (2014). Synchronized metronome training induces changes in the kinematic properties of the golf swing. *Sports Biomech*; 13(1):1-16.

Spasic M, Krolo A, Zenic N, et al. (2015). Reactive agility performance in handball; development and evaluation of a sport-specific measurement protocol. *J Sports Sci Med*; 14(3):501-506.

Spiteri T, Nimphius S, Hart NH, et al .(2014). Contribution of strength characteristics to change of direction and agility performance in female basketball athletes. *J Strength Cond Res*; 28(9):2415-23.

Sporiš G, Milanović L, Jukić I, et al. (2010). The effect of agility training on athletic power performance. *Kinesiology*; 42(1):65-72.

Starosta W. (2006). The concept of modern training in sport. *Stud Phys Cult Tour*; 13(2):9-25.

Stølen T, Chamari K, Castagna C, et al. (2005). Physiology of soccer: an update. *Sports Med*; 35(6):501-36.

Stoyanova S, Ivantchev N, Petrova K. (2016). Spatial orientation in sportsmen. *Europ Scient J*; 12(24):88-96.

Taube W, Kullmann N, Leukel C, et al. (2007). Differential reflex adaptations following sensorimotor and strength training in young elite athletes. *Int J Sports Med*; 28(12): 999-1005.

Taube W, Gruber M, Gollhofer A. (2008). Spinal and supraspinal adaptations associated with balance training and their functional relevance. *Acta Physiol (Oxf)*; 193(2):101-16.

Trecroci A, Milanović Z, Rossi A, et al. (2016). Agility profile in sub-elite under-11 soccer players: is SAQ training adequate to improve sprint, change of direction speed and reactive agility performance? *Res Sports Med*; 24(4):331-340.

Vogel JJ, Bowers CA, Vogel DS. (2003). Cerebral lateralization of spatial abilities: a meta-analysis. *Brain Cogn*; 52(2):197-204.

Wei G, Zhang Y, Jiang T, et al. (2011). Increased cortical thickness in sports experts: a comparison of diving players with the controls. PLoS One; 6(2):e17112.

Verkhoshansky YV.(2006). Special strength training. A practical manual for coaches. Muskegon (MI): Ultimate Athlete Concepts.

Williams LR, Walmsley A. (2000). Response timing and muscular coordination in fencing: a comparison of elite and novice fencers. *J Sci Med Sport*.;3(4):460-75.

Wing AM, Doumas M, Welchman AE. (2010). Combining multisensory temporal information for movement synchronisation. *Exp Brain Res*; 200(3-4):277-82.

Yarrow K, Brown P, Krakauer JW. (2009). Inside the brain of an elite athlete: the neural processes that support high achievement in sports. *Nat Rev Neurosci*;10(8):585-96.

Young WB, Miller IR, Talpey SW.(2015). Physical qualities predict change-of-direction speed but not defensive agility in Australian rules football. *J Strength Cond Res*; 29(1):206-12.

Zachopoulou E , Mantis K, Serbezis V, et al.(2000). Differentiation of parameters for rhythmic ability among young tennis players, basketball players and swimmers. *Europ J Phys Education*; 5(2):220-30.

Zech A, Hübscher M, Vogt L. et al. (2010). Balance training for neuromuscular control and performance enhancement: a systematic review. J Athl Train. 45(4):392-403.

Zemková E.(2009). Balance readjustment after different forms of exercise: A review. *Intern J Appl Sports Sci*; 21(1):45-60.

Zetou E, Vernadakis N, Tsetseli M, et al.(2012). The effect of coordination training program on learning tennis skills. *Sport J*; 15:1-7.

42854181R00090

Made in the USA
Middletown, DE
20 April 2019